the Barbecue America

COOKBOOK

America's best barbecue recipes
from coast to coast.

D1469605

Copyright © 2002 by Rick Browne

ALL RIGHTS RESERVED. No part of this book may be reproduced or
transmitted in any form by any means, electronic or mechanical,
including photocopying and recording, or by any information storage
and retrieval system, except as may be expressly permitted by the 1976
Copyright Act or in writing from the publisher. Requests for permission
should be addressed to The Globe Pequot Press, PO Box 480,
Guilford, CT 06437.

The Lyons Press is an imprint of The Globe Pequot Press

Printed in the United States of America

10 9 8 7 6 5 4 3 2 1

Design by Sandy Fry Design, Portland, OR
Additional book design by Lynn F. Anderson, Portland, OR

Library of Congress Cataloging-in-Publication data is available on file.

the Barbecue America

COOKBOOK

America's best barbecue recipes
from coast to coast.

The Lyons Press
Guilford, CT 06437
www.lyonspress.com
The Lyons Press is an imprint of The Globe Pequot Press

CONTENTS

Up in Smoke

The Authors' Pilgrimage Across America

I was 42 before I knew true "Q." Rick was two klicks shy of a half-century.

We take no pride in this confession. We simply state it by way of explaining how two otherwise sane working journalists started on a bizarre journey over three years across thousands of heartland miles to the core of America's only indigenous cuisine. Before it started, we didn't know barbecue; we didn't know the crazy, charming, giving, irascible, gifted, hilarious, corny, cunning people who make it happen. Heck, we didn't even know each other.

Then again, we both had deprived childhoods. I grew up in Connecticut, where barbecue was any meat cooked outdoors, especially if you slathered on store-bought sauce before you let the flames char it hard and dry. I don't know what crime this is, but I now know that meat wasn't barbecue. Rick was born in Ontario, Canada, of all places, not exactly a barbecue bastion. His first barbecue was a hamburger scorched black and about as tasty as a hockey puck, which is just what he used it for. He was in Canada, eh?

For me, it all started when, as a senior editor for a travel magazine, I took a trip to Hot Springs, Arkansas, thinking I was going to tour bathhouses. Instead I got waylaid in a place called McClard's Bar-B-Q (505 Albert Pike; 501-624-9586), which I visited because I heard it was one of Bill Clinton's favorite joints while growing up in nearby Hope. Greeted by the smell of hickory fumes, I wandered into the unassuming '40s-style family restaurant, ordered a combination plate and my life changed forever. In no time, I was tearing the meat from ribs and scarfing up mouthfuls of beef and pork that had been slow-smoked over the pit for hours. Where I could, I crammed in spicy beans and pungent coleslaw. Unlike Bill Clinton, I freely admit that I inhaled McClard's smoky offerings.

Then I took a fateful trip west into the land of "Q." Rick Browne, the photographer on the story, came east from the Golden State. Rick and I were assigned to write and produce a story about Kansas City, Missouri, (a meat Mecca of revered steakhouses blessed with 75 barbecue restaurants).

We gleefully gnawed, smacked, and salivated our way across the city until someone took a look at my tomato- and molasses-smudged clothes and my partner's camera bag stuffed with "doggie bags" of ribs and brisket—"for later"—and said: "You know, if you want really good 'Q,' you should go to a contest."

"You're kidding. There are contests? Can we eat there?"

"You bet you can, boys."

The next day, we drove across the state line into Kansas for the Great Lenexa Barbecue Cookoff. Our first indication of the size of the smoke-and-spice cult came when we were forced to park a mile from the event and shuttle in with other believers. One was a judge who explained that you learn to pace yourself, taking only a small bite of each or you'd be full in no time. A 10-year-old boy asked to describe the strangest thing he had ever tasted said, "I ate something a couple of years ago, somebody said it might be grizzly bear, but that's supposed to taste like snow tire, and this was better than that."

The night before, 160 contestants had started smoking delicacies that wouldn't be consumed until at least noon that day. They had set up shop around their pits—many homemade contraptions fashioned from oil drums, old industrial washing machines or materials even more bizarre—and smoked cuts of meat in preparation for blind taste tests by 100 judges. They had tended fires, adding wood chunks here, choking the vent a bit there, adding secret elixirs. Sleeping in shifts, they waited by ember glow in a ritual of checking thermometers, trading grill lies, opening beers and just watching.

This idyllic image lost some of its gravity, however, in the light of day. Jacques Strapp and his Supporters (he's a mortgage banker) were cooking in a freezer converted to a smoker. The Bum Steers cooked a pig in a coffin. A team of IBM execs worked under the banner "I Burnt Mine—Burning the Best Bytes Since 1988." However serious these guys (and ladies) were about their "Q," they were there to have fun.

We were instantly captivated by these legions of dedicated barbecuers who had created a wonderful little culinary subculture oblivious to whichever foreign cuisine had just taken New York by storm or which movie star had teamed with which interior designer and which chef to create some "fabulous space" in Tribeca or Rodeo Drive. For dedicated thousands, this was great American eating and they had built their leisure lives

"You know, if you want really good 'Q,' you should go to a contest."

"You're kidding. There are contests? Can we eat there?"

"You bet you can, boys."

around it. This was their bass boat, their country-club membership, their Porsche all rolled into one. Some of these guys had done sailboats, now they were doing barbecue. It was a world of fun. They created names for themselves—"noms de grille," if you will, like the Baron of Barbecue or the Flower of the Flames. They dressed up in costumes and traded stories and told silly jokes. They welcomed strangers in with a "come on in and set a spell; would you like a beer?" charm that was totally engaging to someone who couldn't even get a decent reservation for lunch in my hometown.

But most of all, they had some of the greatest food in the world. We found that out right there in Lenexa. We humbly approached the grill of Karen Putnam, where the decorated cook was giving away meat she had deemed not good enough for competition. Reverently stepping up to the proffered tray of ribs prepared with a "Hollywood cut"—a showman's trick that leaves the most meat possible on either side of the bone—I took communion. I cupped my hands, half expecting her holiness to place the host in them. Instead, I jerked a rib off the tray and into my craw, sucked in a tender mouthful of pork, and nearly sank to my knees.

Co-author and photographer Rick Browne with fellow judge Dorothy Mengering (better known as Dave Letterman's mom) take a break at the Jack Daniel's Invitational.

Hallelujah! The taste of pig and smoke and spice and sauce, all comingling in meat so tender I hardly needed teeth to eat it. I pressed it to the roof of my mouth with my tongue, savoring the complexity of flavor. What was that fruit—raspberry, plum, orange—swimming in the sauce? Were cayenne, paprika, brown sugar, nutmeg peppered in the meat? My eyeballs started floating and I thought to myself: "I'm home at last!"

Rick was off with "The Meatheads" (a.k.a. Ernie and Phyllis Green), a delightful couple who had just won the pork shoulder contest and were celebrating. "Have some butt," Ernie offered. His camera in one hand, a steaming slab of pork shoulder in the other, Rick described the next few moments as the epiphany of his culinary existence. "Suddenly there was a light in the sky, the earth stood still, flavors that I didn't know existed coursed through my mouth—fire and smoke and hickory and oak. I became converted in an instant." He put down the camera and ate with both hands, surely a sign of a future barbecue disciple.

We rushed to buy *Smoke & Spice* by Cheryl Jamison and Bill Jamison (Harvard Common Press, 1994) and the Kansas City Barbecue Society's own *Barbecue…It's Not Just for Breakfast*

Anymore. Then we returned to our homes in New York and California, where we preached barbecue to anyone who would listen. We were zealots of barbecue. We'd call each other once a week to brag.

But even as we learned to slow-roast at low temperatures for optimum smoke and tenderization, we became scourges of our wives' kitchens. Armed with hundreds of recipes, we'd fill the sinks with dirty dishes. Suddenly we were mixing spices, rubs, powders, marinades, sauces and mops for each meat. Strange new stains marred the counters and floors. The freezer filled up with racks of ribs, pork shoulders and beef briskets. Concoctions with scribbled labels such as "cranberry bourbon sauce" or "hotter than hell rub" littered the place. Utensils were broken, pans burnt, meat thermometers obliterated with soot. Rick bragged about his meat thermometer, which cost him $85, being used in a smoker that cost him $29.

When spring came, we burned to continue our education back in the land of "Q." And then one of us—in retrospect, neither one will take the blame, er, credit—came up with the bright idea that if we did a book about barbecue we could tour all of the shrines of barbecue all in the guise of work. We would write a cookbook—but not just a book of recipes and techniques, but a travel guide to barbecue with photographs that would capture the spirit and humor of America's culinary answer to jazz, an original art form.

Soon we were on pilgrimages to many strange lands: Owensboro, Kentucky; Memphis, Tennessee; Fort Bragg, California; Lynchburg, Tennessee; Arlington, Texas and Kansas City, Missouri.

As well as enjoying some of the best eats of our lives (both at contests and the roadside stands we insisted on visiting), we learned a thing or two. We learned that barbecuers are some of the friendliest, most generous people in the world. We learned that everybody has his own opinion about what makes good barbecue. And so we learned something about cooking as well, and that is the other purpose of this book: to share the recipes and techniques we picked up from the experts. If you come away from reading this with a smile and the ability to smoke some "Q" that will make your neighbors sit up and take notice, we've done our job.

Jack Bettridge, co-author, casts a skeptical look at a pork entry at the Jack Daniel's Invitational.

9

INTRODUCTION

The Informed and Informal History of "Q"

Spanish conquistadors, bored with or hungry from a steady regimen of conquering, pillaging and religious converting, one day paused long enough to sniff the sweet aroma of spicy meat and burning wood wafting through the air on some unknown Caribbean island.

Probably Vasco turned to Francisco and said, "What's that sweet smell, man?"

And Francisco replied, "It's coming from one of those green-stick grills. The natives call it a babracot."

"Barbracoa?" Vasco asked.

Francisco agreed that that pronunciation was close enough. Caucasian tongues kept bending the term around until today we have barbecue: a noun, a verb, a food, a party, a restaurant, a way of life.

At least, that's how one story goes about how barbecue was "discovered." There are several, but that's the one that has gained the most credence—based upon its acceptance by that purportedly unimpeachable authority of all things linguistic, the Oxford English Dictionary (OED). But because we seriously doubt the barbecuing experience of the editors of the OED and since it seems even BBQ-scarfing presidents can be impeached these days, we're going to tell you some other stories that just may be lies. And when it comes to BBQ, telling lies has never been an impeachable offense.

Men are more likely than women to barbecue (61% to 39%), but women are more likely to decide what to barbecue (57% to 40%).

The aforementioned OED dismisses as absurd conjecture that the word comes from the French *barbe à queue*, meaning from beard to tail—that is, cooking the whole hog. It may be absurd, but we like this one as it conjures up such pretty pictures of pigs roasting on a spit. What may seem most absurd about this tale is that Frenchmen bothered to think it up at all, since cooking meat on such a scale is not what we've come to expect at Gaulic restaurants named Chez so-and-so, with supercilious waiters running around trying to get you to order meat sliced down to something called medallions. Then again, maybe that's why the theory makes so much sense to the legions that believe it. Often, things get named for aspects that are most remarkable to the people doing the naming. Imagine the Frenchman's horror at such a barbaric pigout: "Beard to tail! Outré!"

Perhaps the most absurd (but oddly appropriate) stories come from tall-tale Texans. One claimed to have coined the term when he decided his "Q" was so delicious he set out a shingle and imprinted it with the name of his ranch: Bar-B-Q. Another variation purports to come from a combination bar, beef eatery and billiards hall that put all of those attributes in its name, shortening bar, beef and cue stick, and coming up with bar-be-cue. Of course, these theories discount the fact that the word was in existence long before there were ranchers or pool joints in Texas, but they do capture a lot of the spirit of "Q"—lie-swapping, one-upmanship and creative naming.

Whatever your favorite story about the name, it's obvious that people slow-smoked meat outdoors ages before there was a term for it. Certainly, that's what the cave dwellers did with fire when they first tamed it. It wasn't until chimneys and ovens (and houses) were invented that you could do much else. Presumably, Europeans were so enamored of the convenience of baking and boiling indoors that they lost the art of barbecue and had to be reintroduced to it over here. Our Native American forefathers never misplaced it to begin with.

At any rate, nobody was about to lose such an art twice. Barbecue caught on with white settlers and mutated with sublime effect as they migrated through North America. Each region they elbowed their way into put its mark on the art in terms of food and fuel. That tradition persists today. Barbecuers typically cook what's raised in the region and smoke with the wood available.

The Spanish explorer Hernando De Soto had already introduced hogs to Florida and Alabama in the 16th century and, at the dawn of the 17th century, English settlers brought pork to Jamestown (no wonder Pocahontas was so attached to John Smith). Being particularly suited to the landscape of the South, swine made their way throughout the region as a food staple. The abundant hickory provided the smoke.

In Texas, first Hispanic and later Anglo ranchers barbecued the cattle they raised with the mesquite trees that grew there. Even later, German immigrants to the hill country would

Americans light up their barbecues 2.9 billion times a year.

add their expertise in butchering, smoking and sausage-making to the mix. They also helped develop the Texans' penchant for cuts such as skirt steak (fajitas) and flank steak.

In New England, a different form of barbecuing (although it wasn't called that) went on at clambakes.

In the Pacific Northwest, natives had already developed a pretty good smoking tradition by the time Europeans arrived. So proficient had they become at catching salmon, which ran in abundance, that local Indians could smoke enough fish to preserve for later consumption and spend the bulk of the year carving totem poles.

As society and civilization evolved in America, so did barbecue become somewhat more civilized and social. George Washington, while he probably never slept at one, mentions going to a "barbicue" in Alexandria, Virginia, in his diary. The first barbecue events probably grew out of the celebration that went along with pig slaughtering. Serious enough were these soirees that the state of Virginia was obliged to pass a law against firing a gun at a barbecue.

Of course, these first barbecues were a little more involved than what many of us are used

to today. Typically, the cooks would dig a pit, chop down trees, burn them into charcoal overnight and then cook for dozens or hundreds of people. In the South, much of this work inevitably fell to the slaves, so blacks became some of the most accomplished pitmasters in the barbecue world, a tradition that continues to this day.

The first swine of the South were not the porcine porkers that we know today, but rather slighter, stringier versions that inspired Arkansans to call them razorbacks. As breeding for meat production became more and more successful, the stature of the lowly pig improved. By the 19th century, barbecue events were the rage among plantation folk.

In fact, Scarlett O'Hara met Rhett Butler at a barbecue in *Gone With the Wind*. Margaret Mitchell describes the petulant Scarlett as she prepares for the event, hoping to wear a

Three out of
four American
households own
barbecue grills.

dress that, her maid assures her, breaks a social code forbidding showing one's bosom before 3 p.m. (not a problem anymore at many barbecues) and arguing that she shouldn't be forced to eat before the party (again, not an untenable position). Miss O'Hara arrives to the "savory aromas of burning hickory logs and roasting pork and mutton" as the meat turns on spits above embers. The barbecue, held next to the rose garden, included linen tablecloths and chairs from the plantation house, and guests were served on silver trays. A separate barbecue was held behind the barn for the black servants.

Being so closely related to the South, barbecue has always been affected by segregation. Sometimes it helped overcome it as the races found common ground in the succulent food. There is a long tradition of whites ignoring their own self-imposed color barriers in order to seek out the best barbecue. Appetite always trumped prejudice. And many of the first anti-segregation lawsuits would be fought in attempts to integrate barbecue joints. Martin Luther King Jr. often met with his compatriots at barbecue restaurants. Bobby Seale, Black Panther Party organizer and 1960s revolutionary, later wrote a book, *Barbeque'n with Bobby*, in which he argues about the spelling of the word and prints a "Barbeque Bill of Rights."

The world's highest barbecue contest is held in the Rocky Mountain town of Frisco, Colorado, 70 miles west of Denver.

Politics and barbecue have a long history as bedfellows in the United States. Office seekers, especially in the Midwest, soon figured out there was almost no better way to draw voters out to rallies than the come-hither smell of smoking meat. This fact is not lost by today's politicians—even on presidential candidates. Lyndon Johnson hosted elaborate spreads he would regularly throw at the LBJ ranch. His pitmaster, Walter Jetton, went on to write the LBJ *Barbecue Cookbook*. Jimmy Carter threw barbecue luncheons on the White

House lawn. Ronald Reagan invited Honey Monk, of Lexington Barbecue No. 1, to cook at the 1983 Economic Summit. Bob Kerrey and Al Gore have competed in the Memphis in May barbecue contest. The congressional representatives of North Carolina and South Carolina regularly battle over "Q." Bill Clinton is a devotee of McClard's BBQ in Hot Springs, Arkansas.

Like Forrest Gump, "Q" was on hand at most of the great moments in American history. The first drive-in restaurant was a barbecue joint. America's other original art form, jazz, matured with barbecue in smoky Kansas City clubs, where the corpulent likes of Charlie Parker chowed down. Packaged charcoal is a by-product of Henry Ford's factory system. It seems old man Ford hated to see the chunks of wood used in manufacturing go to waste and charged his brother-in-law, E. G. Kingsford, with the finding of a use for them. The bags of briquettes were sold by Ford dealers until the 1950s.

In the 20th century, barbecue joints became part of the landscape as pitmasters who were particularly adept found they could make a little cash on the side by selling the products of their grills. Typically, "Q" was sold from a stand outside the home that might be closed on weekdays when the pitmaster was working his regular job or on Sundays if he were particularly religious. The casual approach of these little bistros is a tradition that continues today, when the typical barbecue is likely to be described as a hole in the wall where the menu includes only one or two items. Joints generally follow regional styles: mutton in Kentucky; beef in Texas; vinegar sauces in eastern Carolinas; tomato sauces in the West; Kansas City serves it all.

After World War II, cooking outdoors at home took off as a cultural phenomenon. But unfortunately lost in the exchange were the basic concepts of the art, which even the United States Department of Agriculture knows enough about to describe as "the direct action of heat resulting from the burning of hardwood or the hot coals therefrom for a sufficient period to assume the usual characteristics." Barbecue became Buffy and Chip entertaining on the patio on summer evenings and searing the hamburgers. The final insults were the "go-to-hell" pants with tiny whales all over them and the "kiss-me, I'm-the-cook" aprons.

In the 1970s, orthodox slow-smoking barbecue staged a comeback against the quick-charring methods that appropriated the name in the 1950s. Cookoffs cropped up around the country. Each practiced a local form of the true belief, usually based on readily available meat and fuel. Then in 1978, Memphis in May, the world's largest contest, came into being, followed soon after by American Royal, in Kansas City, considered the World Series of barbecue with its invitational and open competitions. In 1985, the movement had become so huge and the demand for competition information and standardized rules so great that Carolyn and Gary Wells and Rick Welch decided over cocktails to form the Kansas City Barbecue Society (KCBS) to regulate the action.

The pig is a constantly evolving animal. Today's porker has 31 percent less fat, 17 percent fewer calories and 10 percent fewer calories from fat than swine of old.

Marinades & Rubs

Pork 'n' Brew Marinade

12 ounces dark beer
$\frac{1}{2}$ cup vegetable oil
2 tablespoons wine vinegar
1 teaspoon onion powder
1 teaspoon garlic powder
$\frac{1}{2}$ teaspoon paprika
$\frac{1}{2}$ teaspoon salt
$\frac{1}{2}$ teaspoon ground black pepper

Combine all the ingredients in a saucepan. Simmer for 10 minutes over low heat. Good for beef as well as pork. May also be used as a mop. *Makes about 2 cups.*

Big Game Marinade

2 cups dry red wine
$\frac{1}{4}$ cup balsamic vinegar
$\frac{1}{4}$ cup extra virgin olive oil
6 bay leaves
3 garlic cloves, crushed
1 teaspoon salt
1 shot glass tequila
1 tablespoon lime juice
1 teaspoon dried rosemary leaves

Combine all the ingredients (except the rosemary) in a blender and mix well. Place liquid mix in a bottle, add the rosemary and seal tightly. Put in a cold, dark place for 2 to 3 hours to distribute the flavors. Use within 24 hours on beef steaks, ribs, brisket or roasts, venison, bear or elk steaks. *Makes about $2\frac{1}{2}$ cups.*

Serve with a hearty Merlot, Cabernet Sauvignon or Chianti.

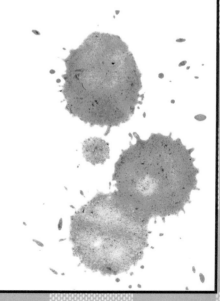

Bird Cookin' Dust

$\frac{1}{4}$ cup salt

3 tablespoons brown sugar

2 tablespoons ground white pepper

1 tablespoon garlic salt

1 tablespoon paprika

1 tablespoon chili powder

1 teaspoon red pepper

1 teaspoon granulated sugar

1 teaspoon onion powder

1 teaspoon ground cumin

1 teaspoon grated lemon zest

Combine all the ingredients. Use on poultry: lightly brush bird with olive oil, then rub spice mixture over and under the skin. Let marinate for up to 12 hours. *Makes about $\frac{3}{4}$ cup.*

WARNING: DO NOT reuse leftover rub or marinade after it has been applied to meat or poultry; it may contain harmful bacteria.

Uncle John's Fruit Marinade Spread

1 cup fruity white wine

$\frac{1}{4}$ cup rice wine vinegar

$\frac{1}{4}$ cup extra virgin olive oil

1 mango, seeded

1 small papaya, seeded

2 teaspoons honey

1 teaspoon salt

1 teaspoon ground white pepper

Juice of 1 medium lemon

Combine the ingredients in a blender and mix well. Transfer to a saucepan and cook over low heat until most of the liquid is gone and you have a very moist paste. Use immediately to coat fish, chicken, game hens or duck. Marinate for 3 to 4 hours. Wipe most of the fruit paste off the surface and smoke or grill. *Makes about $3\frac{1}{2}$ cups.*

John Angood, Battle Creek, Michigan
John is married to Kathy, my old English teacher. John is a superb cook, a talented wood carver and a great friend.

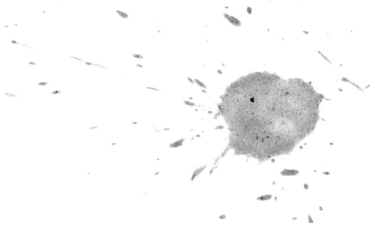

Cuba Libre Marinade

12 ounces cola
1 jigger dark rum
2 scallions, finely chopped
2 tablespoons vegetable oil
Juice of 1 small lime

Combine all the ingredients in a saucepan. Heat on low, being careful not to burn off rum. Cola makes it a very effective and quick (1 to 4 hours) tenderizer. May also be used as a mop. *Makes about $1\frac{3}{4}$ cups.*

Manhattan Marinade

$1\frac{1}{2}$ cups bourbon
$\frac{1}{4}$ cup sweet vermouth
1 tablespoon maraschino cherry juice
1 tablespoon vegetable oil
1 teaspoon onion powder
Dash Angostura bitters

Combine all the ingredients. Shake or stir well. May also be used as a mop. *Makes about $1\frac{3}{4}$ cups.*

Drunken Appul Whiski Marry-nade

2 cups apple juice
1 cup fresh apple cider
1 cup Jack Daniel's sippin' whiskey
1 Golden Delicious or McIntosh apple, minced
$\frac{1}{2}$ cup minced sweet onion
$\frac{1}{2}$ cup sugar
1 tablespoon concentrated lemon juice
1 teaspoon Worcestershire sauce
1 teaspoon salt
1 teaspoon ground white pepper
1 generous shot glass Jack Daniel's

Combine all the ingredients (except the last one) in a saucepan and mix well. Simmer over very low heat for 10 to 15 minutes to mix flavors. Put meat in a sealable plastic bag and cover with half of the sauce, reserving the other half to serve at the table. Is heavenly on pork shoulder and ribs, and a delight on shark or swordfish.

Oh yeah. Pour the shot glass of JD into a glass and sip while you cook. *Makes about 5 cups.*

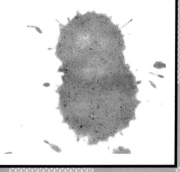

Hot? You Want It Hot?

Variety of Pepper	Scoville Heat Unit
Habanero or Scotch Bonnet	200,000 – 300,000
African Birds-Eye	150,000
Chiltecpin (Round)	70,000
Tabasco	30,000 – 50,000
Chilipiquin (Long)	40,000
Cayenne	35,000
Serrano	10,000 – 25,000
Jalapeño	3,500 – 7,000
Poblano	2,500 – 3,000
Anaheim	1,000 – 1,500
Bell Peppers, Pimentos	0

Scoville Heat Units are measured by diluting the oil of a pepper with water. Then additional water is added until the heat of the pepper can no longer be detected by tasting. For example, oil of cayenne peppers requires 35,000 units of water added to one unit of oil before the "heat" is gone.

Tee-Many Mar-Toonis Marinade

2 cups gin or vodka
$\frac{1}{2}$ cup dry vermouth (less for dry martini lovers)
$\frac{1}{4}$ cup olive oil
2 teaspoons thyme
2 teaspoons onion powder
2 teaspoons rock salt
Juice of 1 large lemon
1 bay leaf

Combine the ingredients. Shake or stir. Most effective with chicken and fish. May also be used as a mop. *Makes about 3 cups.*

Rib Ticklin' Marinade

$\frac{1}{4}$ cup soy sauce
$\frac{1}{4}$ cup vinegar
2 tablespoons sugar
2 tablespoons yellow mustard
2 tablespoons vegetable oil
1 tablespoon ketchup
1 teaspoon cayenne pepper
$\frac{1}{4}$ teaspoon Tabasco Sauce

Combine the ingredients in a saucepan. Bring to a boil, and quickly reduce heat to a simmer. Simmer, covered, for 5 minutes. May also be used as a mop. *Makes about 1 cup.*

Red-Eyed Meat Marinade

2 cups very strong black coffee
1 large onion, chopped into large pieces
1 cup soy sauce
1 cup dry white wine
$\frac{1}{2}$ cup orange juice
$\frac{1}{2}$ cup molasses
1 teaspoon salt
1 teaspoon ground black pepper

Mix the ingredients in a blender. Place in a Mason jar or ceramic bowl and cover. Use as a marinade on pork butt, rib-eye steaks, prime rib or beef brisket. *Makes about 6 cups.*

Soda Jerk

$\frac{1}{4}$ cup onion powder

$\frac{1}{4}$ cup garlic flakes

2 tablespoons baking soda

2 tablespoons freshly ground black and/or white
    and red peppercorns

2 teaspoons cayenne pepper

2 teaspoons Jamaican allspice

2 teaspoons ground cinnamon

2 teaspoons ground nutmeg

2 teaspoons brown sugar

1 teaspoon dried sage

1 teaspoon dried thyme

1 teaspoon dried marjoram

$\frac{1}{4}$ teaspoon ground habanero or Scotch
    bonnet peppers

Mix the ingredients and place in a jar that can be
tightly sealed. Store in the coolest, darkest place
in the house. Use with caution, especially if you've
used Scotch bonnet peppers. Great for beef, pork
or goat dry marinades. *Makes about 1 cup.*

Rick Browne, co-author & photographer
On a trip to the Caribbean for Islands magazine with
writer Jim Gullo, we found this Jamaican jerk recipe at a
small roadside stand on the way to Kingston. A three-
and-a-half-hour journey through hell, the trip resulted in
some great pictures, a story about a part of Jamaica
tourists seldom see and the hottest rub I've ever tasted.

Mops, sops and slathers is not the
name of a law firm. The words
describe different ways of applying
sauces and marinades in cooking.

Sweet-and-Spicy Hickory Rub

1 cup brown sugar
$\frac{1}{2}$ cup hickory salt
$\frac{1}{2}$ cup celery salt
$\frac{1}{2}$ cup paprika
$\frac{1}{2}$ cup ground black pepper
1 tablespoon onion powder
1 tablespoon garlic powder
2 teaspoons cayenne pepper

Mix all the ingredients. Store in a spice container for rubbing on beef and pork. *Makes about 3 cups.*

Chili Con Carnage

$\frac{1}{4}$ cup chili powder
$\frac{1}{4}$ cup paprika
2 tablespoons salt
1 tablespoon oregano
1 teaspoon coriander
1 tablespoon cumin

Mix all the ingredients and use for beef or pork. Store remainder for later use. *Makes about $\frac{3}{4}$ cup.*

Brisket Rub

$\frac{1}{2}$ cup paprika
2 tablespoons brown sugar
2 tablespoons chili powder
2 tablespoons onion powder
$\frac{1}{4}$ cup yellow mustard

Combine paprika, brown sugar, chili powder and onion powder. Mix well. Coat brisket with mustard and sprinkle rub on generously. *Makes about $\frac{3}{4}$ cup.*

Bacon to Basics Rub

$\frac{1}{4}$ cup bacon bits
2 tablespoons paprika
1 tablespoon onion powder
1 tablespoon garlic powder
1 teaspoon chili powder

Crush bacon bits and mix with the rest of the ingredients. Store and use on chicken cuts. *Makes about $\frac{1}{3}$ cup.*

When using thin mops, keep them in handy plastic spray bottles and mist your meat instead of pouring the mop on.

A Tad Tuscan Marinade

$\frac{3}{4}$ cup Italian salad dressing
   (the zestier the better)
2 tablespoons prepared salsa
1 tablespoon sugar

Mix the ingredients in a bowl. Keep refrigerated.
May also be used as a mop. *Makes 1 scant cup.*

Sweet Tooth Rub

$\frac{1}{4}$ cup brown sugar
$\frac{1}{4}$ cup granulated sugar
$\frac{1}{4}$ cup paprika
1 tablespoon ground ginger
1 tablespoon ground cinnamon
1 tablespoon ground nutmeg
1 tablespoon onion powder
1 tablespoon garlic powder
1 tablespoon salt

Mix the ingredients in a bowl and store for rubbing on pork or beef cuts. *Makes 1 generous cup.*

Light but Lively Rub

$\frac{1}{2}$ cup celery salt
$\frac{1}{4}$ cup paprika
2 tablespoons garlic salt
2 tablespoons onion powder
$\frac{1}{2}$ teaspoon ground nutmeg
$\frac{1}{2}$ teaspoon ground ginger

Combine the ingredients in a bowl. Store in a spice container for shaking on cuts you don't want too hot, nor too anemic. *Makes 1 cup.*

Hot As Hades Rub

1 cup paprika
$\frac{1}{4}$ cup salt
$\frac{1}{4}$ cup brown sugar
$\frac{1}{4}$ cup crushed red pepper
1 tablespoon garlic powder
1 tablespoon onion powder
1 tablespoon cayenne pepper
1 teaspoon dried basil

Mix the ingredients in a bowl and store in an empty spice container with a sprinkler top. Use for any fur, fish or fowl in need of extra zest. *Makes 2 cups.*

Sweet Piggie Rubbin' Powder

1 cup packed brown sugar
$\frac{1}{2}$ cup paprika
$\frac{1}{2}$ cup garlic or onion salt
$\frac{1}{2}$ cup seasoned salt
2 tablespoons dry mustard
1 tablespoon celery seed
1 teaspoon ground cloves
$\frac{1}{2}$ teaspoon ground nutmeg
$\frac{1}{2}$ teaspoon ground allspice
1 tablespoon lemonade powder

Combine the ingredients and spread in a dry cast-iron skillet. Air-dry in the sun for 4 to 5 hours, stirring often. If it's damp where you live or you're trying this in winter, set the oven at 200°F. When temperature is reached, turn off the stove. Place pan in oven and leave door ajar while mixture dries for 1 to 2 hours.

To use, rub directly into meat and let stand overnight in the refrigerator. Warm to room temperature and smoke for appropriate time. *Makes about $2\frac{3}{4}$ cups.*

Danny "Bluz Boy" Brodsky, Scotts Valley, California
A great golfer, a great jazz guitarist, a superb barbecuer and a world-class friend.

Reward   Reward

LOST PET PIG!!

300lb. Sow & Beloved Family Friend.

Answers to "SQUEALY"

Please Call. Children are devastated.

Heavenly Piglet Barbecue Sauce

2 cups tomato-based barbecue sauce

$\frac{1}{2}$ cup honey

$\frac{1}{4}$ cup molasses

$\frac{1}{4}$ cup packed brown sugar

$\frac{1}{4}$ cup apricot preserves

3 tablespoons cider vinegar

1 teaspoon garlic powder

1 teaspoon coarsely ground black pepper

1 teaspoon ground lemon pepper

1 teaspoon ground red pepper, or season
   to taste

$\frac{1}{4}$ teaspoon powdered hickory smoke

Mix ingredients in a saucepan and cook over low heat for 30 minutes, stirring regularly to blend flavors. Cool and serve, or bottle. Unused sauce can be kept 2 to 3 weeks, if refrigerated. Use as a baste or finishing sauce on pork, chicken or beef. Makes $3\frac{1}{2}$ cups.

Angie Morgan Grant, Memphis, Tennessee
Angie's sauce won third place in the tomato sauce category at the 1998 Memphis in May Barbecue Contest.

Lexington Dip

$2\frac{1}{2}$ cups cider vinegar

1 cup ketchup

$\frac{1}{3}$ cup packed brown sugar

$\frac{1}{3}$ cup granulated sugar

1 tablespoon Worcestershire sauce

1 teaspoon onion salt

1 teaspoon freshly ground black pepper

1 teaspoon Kitchen Bouquet

$\frac{1}{2}$ teaspoon dried minced onion

$\frac{1}{4}$ teaspoon crushed red pepper

$\frac{1}{4}$ teaspoon Tabasco Sauce

Combine ingredients in a saucepan and bring to a boil, then simmer until sugar dissolves. Cook over low heat for 20 to 25 minutes. Stir in 1 to 2 tablespoons when pulling or chopping pork shoulder, mixing well, then serve the remaining sauce on the side at the table. *Makes about 4 cups.*

Dorothy Lawson Browne, Georgetown, D.C.
My mother, Dorothy Lawson Browne, pulled this out of her family recipe box, saying that she hadn't changed it "much" since it was given to her by her grandmother 80 years ago. "Back then, we didn't have Kitchen Bouquet though," she confesses.

Lone Steer Brisket Sauce

About $\frac{3}{4}$ pound beef fat, cut from steaks or brisket
2 cups ketchup
$\frac{1}{2}$ cup lemon juice
$\frac{1}{2}$ cup lime juice
$\frac{1}{2}$ cup bourbon, beer or water
$\frac{1}{2}$ cup packed brown sugar
1 medium onion, chopped
1 tablespoon Hungarian paprika
1 teaspoon celery salt
$\frac{1}{2}$ teaspoon ground red pepper

Chop fat into large chunks and place in a cast-iron skillet over medium heat until there is 1 cup of fat in pan. Discard unmelted fat and fiber. Add remaining ingredients and cover, simmering for 45 minutes to 1 hour. Bottle or put in a sauceboat to pass at the table. *Makes 3 to 4 cups.*

Bill Payton, Waco, Texas
My roommate in college, Bill was a tall-talkin' Texan who taught me the magic of perfect brisket. This recipe was given to him by a pitmaster at a tiny, greasy, smoky and incredibly popular hole-in-the-wall barbecue joint on the outskirts of Fort Worth.

In 1928, a man came to Alex McClard's tourist court (motel) in Hot Springs, Arkansas, but couldn't pay the $10 room fee. Instead, he turned over a family heirloom barbecue sauce recipe. The rest of the story: McClard used the formula and opened one of the region's and country's most famous and popular barbecue shrines.

Moonlite Black Dip

1 gallon water

2 cups cider vinegar

1½ cups Worcestershire sauce

2½ tablespoons lemon juice

½ cup packed brown sugar

3 tablespoons ground black pepper

2 tablespoons salt

1 teaspoon garlic salt

1 teaspoon ground allspice

1 teaspoon onion powder

Mix ingredients in a large pot and bring to a rolling boil, skimming surface, if necessary. Cook over medium heat for 20 minutes then cool. Use as a baste during cooking and as a dip for mutton, lamb or beef. *Makes about 3 quarts.*

Moonlite Bar-B-Que, Owensboro, Kentucky
This recipe was served for years at Moonlite, one of the best barbecue, family-style eating places in America. Here, lunches are legendary.

PacRim Pourin' Sauce

1 cup Chinese hoisin sauce

½ cup Japanese rice wine vinegar

¼ cup Taiwanese soy sauce

¼ cup sesame oil

2 tablespoons sake

1 tablespoon honey mustard

1 tablespoon minced garlic

1 teaspoon ground ginger

¼ teaspoon Chinese five spice powder

Mix ingredients in a saucepan and cook over low heat for 20 minutes. Bottle and let sauce cool. Serve at room temperature. This sauce is especially nice with duck, chicken, game hens or turkey. Or try it on barbecued salmon. *Makes about 2 cups.*

If you want to use a soft drink in a BBQ sauce, don't use diet varieties; they turn bitter when heated.

RB "Q" Sauce

1 cup cola

1 cup tomato sauce

1 can tomato paste

$\frac{1}{2}$ stick ($\frac{1}{4}$ cup) butter (not margarine)

$\frac{1}{2}$ cup Worcestershire sauce

$\frac{1}{2}$ cup packed brown sugar

$\frac{1}{2}$ cup molasses

$\frac{1}{2}$ cup cider vinegar

1 tablespoon maple sugar pepper

1 tablespoon prepared yellow mustard

1 tablespoon chili powder

1 teaspoon summer savory

1 teaspoon onion powder

1 teaspoon garlic salt

$2\frac{1}{2}$ teaspoons balsamic vinegar

1 healthy dash hot sauce or other pepper sauce

Mix the ingredients and cook over low heat, partially covered, in a cast-iron pot or skillet until sauce is thick enough to coat the back of a metal spoon. Serve at room temperature on the side with pork shoulder or ribs, brisket, chicken or beef ribs. *Makes about 3 cups.*

Rick Browne, Vancouver, Washington
Having stolen ideas from the best barbecuers around the country, I settled on this Kansas City-style sweet sauce as my favorite. It goes with anything, is a kick to make and can be sweetened, spiced up or toned down as your taste buds desire. Experiment, have fun with this, empty the cupboards and spice rack. After all, barbecue isn't cordon bleu cooking, it's only barbecue!

The Diddy-Wa-Diddy sauce contest, part of the American Royal Barbecue Contest, was started by Remus Powers (whose real name is Ardie Davis) in 1983 and today is the largest of its kind in the world. A panel of more than 100 judges tastes and rates more than 400 barbecue sauces and 100 dry-rub formulas each year.

ROYAL FLUSH

The World Series of Barbecue

"If it moves, we cook it," says Carolyn Wells, the executive director of the Kansas City Barbecue Society (KCBS), describing the melting-pot atmosphere that every October welcomes the American Royal.

Fifty or 60 judges sit solemnly at picnic tables in an airplane hangar of a building on the outskirts of Kansas City, Missouri. At the top of a scaffolding, maybe 30 feet above the crowd, stands a solitary bearded man dressed in dark pants, white tuxedo shirt, black bow tie, suspenders and a necklace of pig bones, topped with a bowler hat.

It's Remus Powers, Ph.B., the founder of the Diddy-Wa-Diddy sauce contest and framer of the sober oath that all judges must repeat before they can be entrusted to eat communal offerings of barbecue and pass judgment on them. Dr. Powers (a.k.a. Ardie Davis) asks the gathered arbiters of "Q" a few incisive questions: "Can you taste the difference between a McRib sandwich and real barbecue?" When they all answer yes, the good doctor

When it was announced that he won second place in the rib category at the American Royal, Bubba broke into tears: "I can't believe they picked my ribs."

administers the oath, which ends with the words, "I accept my duty so that truth, justice, excellence in barbecue and the American Way of Life may be strengthened and preserved forever."

All right, it isn't exactly the Hippocratic oath, but then again, the American Royal Barbecue Contest isn't as serious as a heart attack, either. Take the streets, for example. The parking lot outside the American Royal Museum (a testament to the livestock industry that helped make Kansas City great in the frontier days) is divided up into lanes with names such as Ribs Road, Meat Street and Pork Place. Then there are the contestants' names: Team Stupid & Friends; Swine Flew (with its wingless airplane cooker with the broken prop); the You Choke 'em We Smoke 'em team; or High-Tech Cookers, the Pyros with a Purpose ("We ain't just blowin' smoke"). Then there are the costumes—a bit premature for Halloween at this early October party. A motif of skeletons and bloody bodies decorates the Haunted House BBQ; a cameraman for a local TV station wears a Frankenstein mask to hide the fact that he's cooking for a rival station's team.

Memphis may have the reputation for throwing the biggest party and guzzling the most beer per "Q" junkie, but the folks in Kansas City never forget to have fun. Witness the slew of pseudonyms (or *noms de grille*, as they call them) that have come out of one area: Karen Putnam, the Flower of the Flames; Paul Kirk, the Baron of Barbecue; and, of course, Remus Powers. Experienced judges broadcast their eminence with T-shirts that read: "Flaming Idiots: I sat on the Supreme Court." There is no shortage of whimsy among the friendly folks who barbecue in Kansas City. Their approach to the Holy Grail of barbecue is ecumenical, almost laissez faire compared with the rest of the known world. Each area of the country seems to have its predilections—and therefore its prejudices. Across the Carolinas, they agree pig (and only pig) should be smoked with hickory, but they argue over sauces, vinegar-based winning out in the East, tomato in the West. In Memphis, some zealots eschew sauce altogether while others demand it. Texans don't consider it barbecue unless mesquite fires beef.

Barbecue judge's oath (delivered with all the seriousness of a church wedding, baptism or presidential inauguration): "I solemnly swear to objectively and subjectively evaluate each barbecue meat that is presented to my eyes, my nose and my palate. I accept my duty so that truth, justice, excellence in barbecue and the American Way of Life may be strengthened and preserved forever."

In Kentucky, they smoke mutton. Each area is convinced their way is the only way to smoke the true "Q." Except Kansas City, where a live-and-let-live spirit prevails. "If it moves, we cook it," says Carolyn Wells, the executive director of the Kansas City Barbecue Society (KCBS), describing the melting-pot atmosphere that every October welcomes the American Royal.

Along with its slew of shrinelike barbecue restaurants, this everything-but-road-kill approach may be what makes Kansas City the capital of the cuisine (don't dare say that in Texas or Memphis or the Carolinas, however). In Kansas City, no one is left out of the mix. If you want to smoke brisket, pork shoulder or chicken, that's all right. Beef ribs, baloney, there's even a place that serves barbecued tofu. That spirit carries over to the American Royal, where you are likely to see whole goat being cooked right next to turkey. Certainly, the predominance of KCBS in its sanctioning of contests in the world of "Q" is partly attributable to the flexible attitudes when it comes to what to cook.

None of this, however, is to suggest that they aren't sincere about their "Q" in Kansas City. Any place where they have 75 barbecue joints to choose from is serious smoking country. A quick walk through the grounds of the American Royal, and that will be clear to even casual observers. Teams toil over their cuts all through the night and jealously guard their secrets. When a stranger wanders by, a woman quickly covers her specially prepared pumpkin soup. "Oh, I thought you were a cooker," she explains when she realizes the interloper is a judge, not a contestant. "You don't know how many recipes I've had stolen from me here."

Kansas City's reputation for barbecue is so respected that some 380 teams make the trek to KC each year to meet and compete. The contest happens over two days and actually comprises two separate main competitions, as well as several side events such as the sauce cookoff. The main events require entrants to cook ribs, pork shoulder, whole hog, chicken, brisket and sausage. The first day is by invitation only, and contestants typically have to win a state contest or other equally prestigious smoke-off during the previous year to be able to enter. The second day is devoted to the open competition, which anyone may enter. The American Royal draws teams from all over the country, from the Pacific Northwest clear across to New England. Many have entered both contests, but none has ever been able to sweep the entire weekend at the American Royal, despite the boasts of the cocky grillmaker Oklahoma Joe,

Kansas City's reputation for barbecue is so respected that some 380 teams make the trek to KC each year to meet and compete. The American Royal draws teams from all over the country, from the Pacific Northwest clear across to New England.

who stood on the bridge of his railroad car cooker after winning the preliminary a few years ago and proclaimed he was going to show KC how to kick butt. We assume he meant pork butt.

And while this kind of braggadocio rolls off the backs of Kansas City barbecuers, this doesn't mean they don't have their own sense of regional pride and one-upmanship. Ernie Green, head of a local team called the Meatheads, takes barbecue seriously enough that he talked his wife, Phyllis, into traveling to a contest in Colorado on their thirtieth wedding anniversary. When, at a recent American Royal contest, two good ol' boys from San Antonio approached him asking for "Q" tips, Ernie told them with a grin, "The best advice we can give to Texans on barbecue is to get on I-35 and head north to Kansas City."

Sunrise BBQ Sauce

1 cup white vinegar

$\frac{3}{4}$ cup yellow mustard

$\frac{1}{2}$ cup water

1 small yellow onion, minced

$\frac{1}{4}$ cup puréed tomatoes

2 tablespoons minced garlic

$2\frac{1}{2}$ teaspoons Hungarian paprika

$1\frac{1}{4}$ teaspoons salt

$\frac{1}{2}$ teaspoon ground white pepper

$\frac{1}{4}$ teaspoon ground red pepper

Mix ingredients in a saucepan and simmer over low heat for 30 minutes, stirring regularly to blend flavors. Cook until the onions are very tender and liquid has reduced by half. Cool and serve. Unused sauce can be kept for 2 to 3 weeks, if refrigerated. Use as a baste or finishing sauce on pork, chicken or beef. *Makes about $1\frac{1}{2}$ cups.*

This sauce is loosely based on the superb sauce served at Maurice's Piggie Park, in West Columbia, South Carolina. Or you can buy the sauce by calling 800 MAURICE and ordering a bottle.

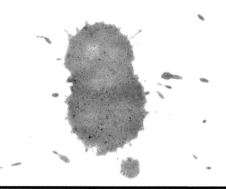

For a tasty and spicy treat: Place one or two habanero or chili peppers in a jar of honey for 2 to 3 weeks. Remove the peppers and you have a spicy condiment to use in barbecue sauces or marinades.

Fractured Béarnaise Sauce

1 large shallot, minced
$\frac{1}{2}$ teaspoon dried tarragon
$\frac{1}{2}$ teaspoon dried basil
2 tablespoons vegetable oil
$\frac{1}{4}$ cup tarragon vinegar
$\frac{1}{4}$ cup cooking sherry
2 tablespoons tomato paste
1 stick ($\frac{1}{2}$ cup) butter
3 egg yolks
$1\frac{1}{2}$ tablespoons lemon juice
Salt
Ground white pepper

Sauté shallot, tarragon and basil in oil in a small saucepan. Add vinegar, sherry and tomato paste. Boil to a paste. Melt half the butter and keep liquid at the ready. Cut remaining butter into tablespoons. Whisk egg yolks and beat into a double boiler, turning constantly over hot water. When eggs are smooth and fluffy, but not scrambled, remove immediately and whisk in cold butter 1 tablespoon at a time. When smooth again, drip in melted butter and lemon juice, whisking continuously. Salt and pepper to taste. Use on grilled beef or poultry. *Makes about 1 cup.*

Our friends all think Béarnaise sauce is too highfalutin for barbecue, so we created this tomato-mixed concoction to put them off the trail, while we enjoy our steaks.

There is a certain barbecue establishment on the outskirts of Nashville that plays a dirty trick on its restaurant competitor across the road. During lunchtime, when cars pull into the lot across from his barbecue pits, the pitmaster pours pork grease on an open bed of coals in front of his restaurant. The resulting pungent, mouth-watering clouds of smoke drift across the street, enveloping the customers of this nationally known fast-food eatery in olfactory heaven. They often locate the source of the tantalizing smoke, hop right back into their cars, drive across the street and chow down on superb barbecue pork shoulder, brisket and chicken.

Old English Sauce

6 ounces pale ale

$\frac{1}{2}$ cup tomato-and-molasses-based barbecue
   sauce

2 tablespoons prepared horseradish

2 tablespoons English mustard

1 tablespoon onion powder

$\frac{1}{4}$ teaspoon ground black pepper

Mix ingredients and use on roast beef. *Makes about $1\frac{1}{2}$ cups.*

Plum Good Sauce

$\frac{1}{4}$ cup packed brown sugar

1 tablespoon ground white pepper

1 tablespoon prepared yellow mustard

1 teaspoon ground cinnamon

1 tablespoon vegetable oil

1 cup ketchup

$\frac{1}{2}$ cup vinegar

$\frac{1}{2}$ cup plum butter

2 tablespoons molasses

Sauté sugar, pepper, mustard and cinnamon in oil. Add ketchup, vinegar, plum butter and molasses, stirring vigorously. Simmer for 30 minutes. Use on game, duck or pork. *Makes about $1\frac{3}{4}$ cups.*

There are more than 760 barbecue sauces bottled in the United States. Some companies will bottle your own recipe in small batches and design labels for you.

BBQ'ed Pork Ribs

1 2-pound slab of pork ribs
1 cup cider vinegar
1 cup white wine
$\frac{1}{4}$ cup balsamic vinegar

Marinate ribs in half of the vinegar-wine mixture overnight in a covered dish in the refrigerator. Place remaining marinade in a plastic spray bottle. Remove ribs and let meat rest until it reaches room temperature. When smoker is up to temperature (220°F to 240°F), place meat in rib rack on grill. Cook for 5 to 6 hours, moistening once an hour with spray bottle of marinade. The ribs are ready when they are fork-tender and have an internal temperature of 180°F.

Serve with your favorite barbecue sauce on the side. *Serves* 4.

In colonial Williamsburg, the Labor Day weekend is celebrated by cooking a whole hog the way 18th-century pitmasters did: basting the hog generously with a mixture of saltwater and melted butter.

Big ol' Whole Hawg

1 dressed whole hog (130 to 150 pounds)
1 quart extra virgin olive oil
1 large apple or orange
2 cups paprika
1 cup freshly ground black pepper
$1\frac{1}{2}$ cups garlic salt
$\frac{1}{2}$ cup chili powder
$\frac{1}{2}$ cup dried summer savory
$\frac{1}{2}$ cup dried oregano
$\frac{1}{2}$ cup onion powder
3 tablespoons ground red pepper
Basting sauce:
1 gallon apple juice
1 gallon cider vinegar
1 pound butter, melted

Trim excess fat from body of dressed hog. Cover snout, tail and ears with aluminum foil and hold in place with toothpicks. Insert large apple or orange into hog's mouth. Rub olive oil into flesh and then work mixed dry spices into flesh. Place hog on smoker, skin side down, rear end toward heat source and cook at 270°F for $4\frac{1}{2}$ hours. Damper fire so heat reduces to 230°F to 240°F. Baste well with sauce and fill cavity with half the remaining sauce; baste every 2 hours for 10 to 12 hours. After 7 hours, turn hog so head is toward heat source. Hog is ready when internal temperature is 170°F. Before serving replace apple or orange with fresh fruit. *Serves* 40-50.

Barbecued Bologna

1 medium onion, chopped
2 tablespoons butter
1 cup tomato sauce
$\frac{1}{4}$ cup clam broth
1 tablespoon dried parsley
$\frac{1}{2}$ teaspoon garlic powder
1 2-pound tube of bologna

Sauté onion in butter. Add tomato sauce, clam broth, parsley and garlic powder. Cook for 5 minutes on low heat. Score bologna to $\frac{1}{8}$ inch throughout. Pour on sauce and let sit for 25 minutes. Bring grill to 250°F. Cook for 90 minutes or until bologna is warm throughout and sauce becomes crusty. *Serves 4-6.*

Smokin' Dogs

Lest we forget as we get so caught up in our rarefied barbecue roots, here's one for the minimalists. Sometimes a barbecue is little more than a cookout.

Plump pork hot dogs
New England-style frank rolls
Yellow mustard
Tomato-based barbecue sauce
Grated cheddar cheese (optional)

Score hot dogs slightly. Place on smoking grill at 300°F. Cook for about 30 minutes. Mix mustard and barbecue sauce as relish. If you're not a purist, slice dogs lengthwise 5 minutes before removing from grill and stuff with cheese.

Country-Style Ribs

4 pounds country-style pork ribs

12 ounces cola

1 jigger dark rum

Juice of 1 small lime

2 scallions, finely chopped

2 tablespoons vegetable oil

2 tablespoons ground mustard

2 tablespoons paprika

2 teaspoons pepper

Country-style ribs (from the blade end of the loin) are the pig's meatiest part, but take some boiling to soften them for the grill. Here is one way to do it:

Cover ribs in a large pot with water. Bring to a boil and simmer 30 minutes. Combine cola, rum, lime, scallions and oil in a saucepan. Heat on low, being careful not to burn off the rum. Use on ribs as a marinade and refrigerate for 2 hours. Mix mustard, paprika and pepper and coat ribs. Grill over medium heat until crisp. Mop often. Serve with a tomato-based sauce. *Serves* 4-6.

Pork spareribs come from the belly of the hog, next to the bacon. They are superb on the barbecue grill because the combination of fat and pork works wonders when slowly smoked.

Quick Butt

$\frac{1}{4}$ cup packed brown sugar

$\frac{1}{4}$ cup granulated sugar

$\frac{1}{4}$ cup paprika

1 tablespoon ground ginger

1 tablespoon ground cinnamon

1 tablespoon ground nutmeg

1 tablespoon onion powder

1 tablespoon garlic powder

1 tablespoon salt

$\frac{1}{2}$ pork butt ($2\frac{1}{2}$ to 3 pounds)

12 ounces cola

1 jigger dark rum

2 scallions, finely chopped

2 tablespoons vegetable oil

Juice of 1 small lime

Two hours before you plan to cook, mix sugars, spices, onion and garlic powders, and salt and rub thoroughly on pork butt. Reserve remaining rub. Refrigerate 1 hour. Mix cola, rum, scallions, oil and lime juice. Pour over pork butt and let stand 1 hour at room temperature, turning several times. Reserve liquid for mop. Prepare grill at 300°F. Cook 2 to 4 hours or until internal temperature reaches 180°F, basting often. Let stand at room temperature for 15 minutes and shred pork for sandwiches. *Serves* 4.

Girded Loins

2 teaspoons ground ginger

1 teaspoon white pepper

$\frac{1}{4}$ teaspoon garlic salt

$\frac{1}{4}$ teaspoon ground cloves

1 3- to 4-pound boneless pork loin

Meat baste:

$\frac{1}{4}$ cup palm or brown sugar

$\frac{1}{4}$ cup soy sauce

$\frac{1}{4}$ cup pineapple juice

Rub spice mixture into meat and marinate for 4 to 6 hours. Place pork loin, fat side up, on grill away from heat. Baste often with sugar-soy-pineapple mixture during cooking time of 2 to $2\frac{1}{2}$ hours. When internal temperature reaches 170°F, place meat in foil and seal tightly. Keep warm until ready to serve. *Serves 4-6.*

Katie's Best Butt

5 tablespoons brown sugar

2 tablespoons paprika

1 tablespoon maple pepper

1 tablespoon lemon pepper

1 tablespoon chili powder

1 tablespoon dried summer savory

2 teaspoons granulated garlic

2 teaspoons seasoned salt

1 teaspoon onion powder

$\frac{1}{4}$ teaspoon crushed red pepper

$\frac{1}{4}$ teaspoon ground cloves

$\frac{1}{4}$ teaspoon ground nutmeg

1 5- to 6-pound pork butt, trimmed

3 cups apple juice

$\frac{1}{2}$ cup apple brandy

Mix all the dry ingredients and rub into the trimmed pork butt. Cover and marinate in the refrigerator overnight, if possible. If not, wait at least 1 hour before cooking. Let meat sit at room temperature for at least 30 minutes before cooking.

Place pork on smoker grill rack over water pan. In water pan you can add sliced apples and oranges for a nice fruity steam. Smoke the meat with lid down over medium coals, turning every hour, for 6 to 8 hours or until bone wiggles easily when pushed. Baste with apple juice and apple brandy mixture after 3 hours at 1-hour intervals when you turn meat. Let meat sit covered for 20 to 30 minutes. Slice, pull or chop meat and serve. *Serves* 6-8.

Katie Welch, Hartford, Connecticut
This recipe was passed down to Katie from her mother, Theresa, who learned to cook barbecue from her grandmother, who emigrated from Hungary to Nashville, Tennessee, in 1905.

Memphis Dry Ribs

2 3-pound (or less) pork rib slabs

Rib rub:

$\frac{1}{2}$ cup paprika

$\frac{1}{2}$ cup garlic salt

$\frac{1}{2}$ cup brown sugar

$\frac{1}{4}$ cup ground black pepper

2 tablespoons chili powder

1 tablespoon dried oregano

Basting spray:

$\frac{1}{2}$ cup olive oil

$\frac{1}{2}$ cup beer

$\frac{1}{4}$ cup lemon juice

1 tablespoon steak sauce

Mix rub ingredients. Use two-thirds of the mixture to rub into ribs. Place in covered pan and refrigerate overnight. Let ribs warm to room temperature and place in smoker (temperature 210°F to 230°F) for 5 to 6 hours, turning once an hour and moistening with basting spray each time you turn them. Take ribs off heat and, after spraying again, sprinkle with the remaining one-third of dry spice mix. Cover tightly in foil and let rest for 20 minutes before serving.

Ribs are perfect served like this, but if your guests prefer, you can serve a favorite barbecue sauce on the side. *Serves* 4-6.

MEMPHIS IN MAY

The Super Bowl of Barbecue

The Memphis in May Barbecue Contest annually serves 39-plus TONS of pork.

"Stop your squealing . . . you're addicted to barbecue," the king says to his queen while he paces the throne room, dressed in regal finery. Swooning with hunger, the queen agrees she's hooked and sings a barbecue testament to the tune of "Good Golly, Miss Molly," complete with Broadway dance steps. They must send off to the New World for meat! Suddenly we're on the open sea and Christopher Colum-b-cue is in search of the Mystic Land of "Q." But here comes Elvis singing "You ain't nothin' but a smoked hog, layin' on a grill." Returning to a nautical theme, Popeye struts by, clamoring for rib-eyes. He's had it with spinach. Just then an iceberg floats by to sink the Titanic. A bevy of Rhett Butlers and Scarlett O'Haras promenade through, and Jake from "The Blues Brothers" belts out "I'm a 'Q' man" to wrap up the action.

Hallucination? Bad dream? A cultural reference Twilight Zone? No, this is the Memphis in May World Championship Barbecue Cooking Contest, and a team called the Adribbers has decided to fete the guest of honor, Portugal, with a little historical skit. The logic may be fractured, but nobody ever accused Memphis in May of being too serious. It's barbecue gone Hollywood. This is Super Bowl week, the Mardi Gras and one King Hell redneck picnic all rolled into one. *The Guinness Book of World Records* certifies that it's the largest contest in the world, but no one needs to verify that it's the wildest cookout what am.

Two hundred fifty teams set up along the Mississippi River front and lay down a mile of smoke for three wondrous days of pork worship. Ninety thousand non-combatants show up as much for the excuse to wear pig snouts, bellow out rebel yells, drink and dance and see once-sane friends make fools of themselves in public as for the chance to sample smoked delicacies. Showmanship, silly skits, booth appearance and, yes, even T-shirt design count right up there with cooking ability when all the votes are tabulated at the end of the day.

All right. The food is fall-off-the-bone delicious—no question—but the real essence of this thing called Memphis in May is the party. At Kansas City's American Royal, the first thing they ask you is where you're from. At the Jack Daniel's Invitational, downstate, they ask you what you're cooking. In Memphis, they ask you what you want to drink. If you're looking for barbecue served up with reverence and solemnity in a pastoral setting, go somewhere else. But if you want to rock your sauce off, Memphis is the place.

It's 10 a.m., and the rock music has already started to pump from a host of competing, expensive stereo systems. Nearly all the teams have filled every inch of real estate allotted them with fancy furnishings and elaborate equipment. Many lots are walled and boast flowered walkways. Most have themes—an Old West storefront stands next to a Hawaiian luau hut. A medieval castle competes with an airport runway. One team has a three-story steel framework with separate tiers for cooking, drinking and dancing. Most sport beer kegs, some daiquiri mixers. Fountains bubble. Cellular phones warble. Not many of the luxuries of home were left there.

Every team's area is based around a common item: the grill. The Smokin'

Ninety thousand non-combatants show up to wear pig snouts, bellow out rebel yells, drink and dance and see once-sane friends make fools of themselves.

This is Super Bowl
week, Mardi Gras, and
one King Hell redneck
picnic all rolled into one.
*The Guinness Book of
World Records* certifies
that Memphis in May is
the largest contest in
the world.

Starlifters, from the Tennessee Air National Guard, has a smoker in the shape of a jet with a GCS (Grease Control System) in case "someone gets drunk and doesn't watch the fire." Oklahoma Joe, a maker of mammoth grills, arrives with a rig the size and shape of a locomotive. The Possum Town Pork Forkers have a 12-foot cooker shaped like a pipe bomb. They made it from stainless steel parts earmarked for toxic waste containers (never used, of course). The guys at the Bryce Boar Blazer put their grill right out front for all to see. It's a glassed-in model with a beer keg split and filled with charcoal under about a dozen chickens. Over a

12-year history, they have developed a reputation for beer butt chicken, a dish smoked with a full can of beer thrust into its body cavity during cooking. Team member Phyllis Lovell offers, "Of course, we've got a whole long story about all the beer from the keg going up into the pig, but there isn't any beer."

Because Memphis in May (and all its sanctioned events) employs on-site judging, fanciful tall tales when describing cooking methods are not only tolerated, they are encouraged. Unlike Kansas City Barbecue Society contests, the teams host judges to a sit-down meal and score points for showmanship. Over the 21 years they have been competing, some teams have gotten pretty fancy as they spin yarns about their barbecue philosophy over tables set with linen and silver. Most offer a choice of fine wines. Alas, judges no longer may sample alcohol at the booths. One was "overserved" a couple of years ago and passed out in her food.

It's fairly easy to tell when the judges are about to show up at Airpork Crew. That's when the partying ends and the cleanup starts to get frenzied. At Airpork Crew, it's a military operation. Team captain Jimmy Johnson cries, "Last call," and everybody goes into action. Hangers-on are ejected. Two vacuum cleaners go over the Astroturf floor, somebody dusts the ceiling fan overhead, and another trencher-man sprays Armor-All on the rubber mat that leads up the walk past the flower boxes and trophies the team has garnered. Soon, everyone's assembled out front, identical in their shorts and team polo shirts. Johnson steps out and asks, "Everybody got their hats on straight? Got their shirts tucked in?"

Johnson's been through this before. The previous year, his team lost out on a chance for the grand prize because one judge scored it one point less than perfect on appearance. "That was a bad judge," he says. "If I cook a shoulder for 22 hours, I don't appreciate getting a bad judge."

When the judges arrive, Airpork Crew is more than ready for them. Johnson shows them to his grill—by now garnished with a slew of fruits and vegetables in a sort of horn-of-plenty pattern. He sweet-talks them a little and then breaks into his philosophy about the membranes that attach the meat to the bone and the proper temperature to heat them to in order to make the meat fall off the bone.

Evidently, the judges don't buy into his culinary thesis, because, when the contest

It's fairly easy to tell when the judges are about to show up. That's when the partying ends and the cleanup starts to get frenzied.

The Sow Luau team keeps papier-mâché pig heads—one for each year of the team's existence—outside its booth. The only problem is occasionally someone takes one as a trophy. "Alcohol knows no fear," smirks one of the team members, shaking his head.

is over, Airpork Crew has won no firsts for cooking. However, their diligence at housework is rewarded. They take first place in the booth contest.

Farther upriver, JR Ribbers is toiling away with no hope of winning a prize. They're professional caterers and have been called upon simply to provide delicious "Q" for the guests of the deep-pocket corporate sponsor who hired them. The irony is that Anthony Morris, who heads the group, is the son of Bessie Louise Cathay, the woman who won the fledgling contest 21 years ago. Morris

remembers calling his mother the night of the event. "I said, 'How are you, Mom?' She said, 'I'm tired from cooking.' I said, 'How did you do?' She said, 'I won.' I didn't believe her. Then I went over and she is sitting in the front room with her legs up in the dark and the trophy sitting there."

Nearby, Roberto Basquez heads a team of Emergency Medical Technicians. He warns that "you don't want to go to the trauma center during Memphis in May because half the people are here cooking." Sobering thought.

Down the path past the Miss Piggy Contest, the Swashbucklers, the Mermaids, the Octopus, the debonair black guy in a white dinner jacket, and the couple dressed like Bill Clinton and Monica Lewinsky—with kneepads on—is Aporkalypse Now. A fun-loving crew of former hunting buddies, they are trying to decide who will enter this year's Hall of Shame. Last year it was the guy who got even with the Kroger's food market team next door. Seems Kroger people had their fountain in the no-decoration zone in front of the booth. So Frank "The Soapmeister" Pickard took a bottle of dishwashing detergent and poured it into the offending fountain. The bubbles ran across the pathway and into the river. Foot traffic was shut down for half an hour. Barbecue history was made that night.

The Sow Luau team keeps papier-mâché pig heads—one for each year of the

team's existence—outside its booth. The only problem is occasionally someone takes one as a trophy. "Alcohol knows no fear," smirks one of the team members, shaking his head.

One team that steadfastly ignores any hooliganism is among the few all-women teams at the contest. Team leader Angie Morgan Grant is a barbecuer on a mission. In honor of her son, she has dedicated her entry to organ-donor programs. Ronald died recently of cystic fibrosis, but only after enjoying a year of life because of a lung donation. She passes out fliers thanking the program for her son's extra year of life and imploring people to become donors.

She reflects about her status as a female contestant and suggests that "sometimes men can get a little on the chauvinistic side, but I'm going to wear their butts out today." Alas, during on-site judging, her rib meat fails to fall off the bone and her dreams seem dashed.

Hours later, she stands watching the awards ceremony anxiously. "This has got to be the toughest part—all the tension," she says. And then it comes. Third place in the tomato sauce contest. Vindication. She can leave this redneck picnic with her head held high, and all is right with Memphis in May.

What do barbecue and caviar have in common? Bland white bread is the medium of choice for both of them.

North Carolina Pork Shoulder

1 14- to 16-pound pork shoulder

Dry marinade:

$\frac{1}{2}$ cup brown sugar

$\frac{1}{4}$ cup paprika

$\frac{1}{4}$ cup garlic salt

2 tablespoons ground black pepper

2 tablespoons onion powder

2 tablespoons chili powder

1 tablespoon ground sage

1 teaspoon dry mustard

$\frac{1}{2}$ teaspoon cayenne pepper

$\frac{1}{2}$ teaspoon dried thyme

Have butcher trim fat from shoulder, leaving a 4-inch portion of fat at the shank (bone) end. Rub well with dry marinade (saving a handful for later), working into every inch of the shoulder. Put in large plastic bag or bowl and cover. Refrigerate for 24 hours. Bring to room temperature and place on cooker, which has been preheated to 220°F. Cook for 11 to 13 hours or until internal temperature is 180°F.

Remove meat from smoker and cool to 140°F. Pull meat from bones and either shred it or chop it and place in a large bowl or glass container. Sprinkle meat with the remaining handful of mixed spices and mix well. Place in foil pouch and seal completely. Serve with buns, coleslaw, pickles, sliced onions and North Carolina-style vinegar-pepper-sugar barbecue sauce. *Serves* 10-12.

Pickin' Picnic

12 ounces dark beer

$\frac{1}{2}$ cup vegetable oil

2 tablespoons wine vinegar

1 teaspoon onion powder

1 teaspoon garlic powder

$\frac{1}{2}$ teaspoon paprika

$\frac{1}{2}$ teaspoon salt

$\frac{1}{2}$ teaspoon black pepper

1 6-pound pork shoulder

1 tablespoon cayenne pepper

1 tablespoon dry mustard

2 tablespoons sugar

The night before you cook, combine beer, oil, vinegar, onion powder, garlic powder, paprika, salt and pepper in a saucepan. Heat for 10 minutes at a simmer. Place pork in resulting marinade and refrigerate overnight, turning several times. In the morning, reserve marinade as mop and rub down pork with cayenne, mustard and sugar. Return pork to the refrigerator for at least 4 hours. Prepare grill to 300°F and smoke pork, mopping liberally. Cook for 2 to 4 hours or until meat reaches internal temperature of 170°F. Set out for 30 minutes and shred meat. Serve in sandwiches. *Serves 6-8.*

Pork Chops

¾ cup Italian salad dressing (the zestier the better)

2 heaping tablespoons applesauce

2 tablespoons prepared salsa

1 tablespoon sugar

Salt and pepper to taste

6 pork chops, 1 inch thick, trimmed

Mix salad dressing, applesauce, salsa, sugar, salt and pepper at least 4 hours before cooking. Thoroughly slather chops with marinade in shallow nonreactive pan. Cover and refrigerate. Reserve excess for mopping. Prepare grill. Smoke chops for 1 hour or until meat thermometer placed in the center reads 160°F. Mop occasionally with remaining marinade. *Serves 4-6.*

The Swine Flew BBQ team cooks in a converted Cessna equipped with a "meat-seeking" missile.

Some o' Dem Chops

6 pork chops, about 2 inches thick

Marinade:

2 cups apple cider

$\frac{1}{4}$ cup fresh orange juice

$\frac{1}{4}$ cup brandy

$\frac{1}{4}$ cup garlic salt

1 tablespoon ground white pepper

$\frac{1}{4}$ cup packed brown sugar

1 tablespoon chili paprika

1 tablespoon dried sage

Place chops and the marinade ingredients in a sealable plastic bag and refrigerate for 4 to 6 hours. Remove chops and reserve liquid. Bring to room temperature. Grill over medium coals until cooked through, turning and basting often with reserved liquid. *Serves* 6.

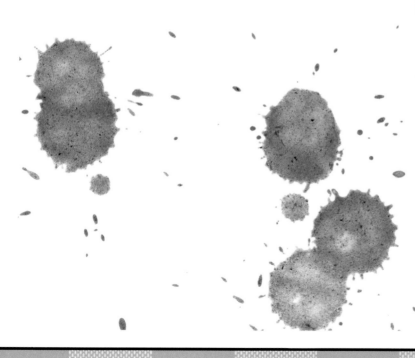

In South Carolina, a "Truth in Barbecue" law makes restaurants put up notices letting customers know if they cook with wood or other fuels and if they cook whole hogs or just part of the hog.

Barbecued Baby Backs

4 baby back rib racks, about
  2 pounds each
2 tablespoons paprika
2 tablespoons seasoned salt
2 teaspoons garlic powder
2 teaspoons onion powder
1 cup beer
1 cup apple juice

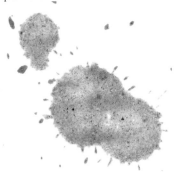

Trim membrane from rib racks. Mix paprika, salt, garlic powder and onion powder. Rub liberally into ribs. Wrap in aluminum foil and place in refrigerator for 4 hours. Prepare smoker to 250°F to 275°F. Place ribs in foil on grill for 2 hours. Remove foil and place ribs on grill for 1 hour away from flame, spraying liberally with beer and apple juice mixture. Coat with favorite sauce and cook for 30 minutes, being vigilant not to let sauce create hard coating.

Baby back ribs (from the center of the loin) are the most delicate the pig has to offer and some care should be used not to cook them too hard and crisp. *Serves 4-6.*

World Championship Barbecue Cooking Contest

May 16, 1998

PAY TO THE ORDER OF The Other Team

$5,000

Five Thousand and 00/100 DOLLARS

Memphis In May International Festival

Poultry

Beer Butt Bird

1 4- to 5-pound chicken

Dry rub:

1 teaspoon palm sugar

1 teaspoon garlic powder

1 teaspoon onion powder

1 teaspoon cayenne pepper

1 teaspoon paprika

1 teaspoon dry yellow mustard

1 tablespoon finely ground sea salt

Basting spray:

1 cup apple cider

1 tablespoon balsamic vinegar

Steaming liquid:

12 ounces of your favorite beer
(canned fruit juice can be substituted)

Wash, dry and season chicken generously inside and out with rub. Work mixture well into skin and under skin wherever possible. Set aside, covered, at room temperature for an hour or so. Drink half the can of beer. Place can on smoker grill and lower chicken onto can so that the legs and can itself hold the chicken upright. This positioning does two things: First, it helps drain off fat as the chicken cooks; second, the beer steams the inside of the chicken, making it the most moist bird you've ever laid yer eyes on.

Smoke 2 to $2\frac{1}{2}$ hours, spraying with basting spray several times, until chicken is done and internal temperature is 180°F for a whole chicken. Carefully remove the bird still perched on the can and place on serving tray. After your guests have reacted appropriately, remove the chicken from can (careful! that aluminum can is very hot, use oven mitts) and carve. *Serves* 4-6.

Dat Ded Bird Thang

1 large chicken (5 pounds or more), butterflied

Dry rub:

1 teaspoon paprika

1 teaspoon dried basil

1 teaspoon seasoned salt

$\frac{1}{2}$ teaspoon maple pepper

$\frac{1}{2}$ teaspoon ground thyme

$\frac{1}{2}$ teaspoon chili powder

$\frac{1}{4}$ teaspoon onion salt

$\frac{1}{4}$ teaspoon cayenne pepper

Baste:

1 cup pineapple juice

$\frac{1}{2}$ cup bourbon or whiskey

$\frac{1}{2}$ cup packed brown sugar

$\frac{1}{4}$ cup concentrated lemon juice

$\frac{1}{4}$ cup steak sauce

$\frac{1}{2}$ cup melted butter

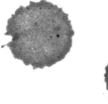

Wash and pat-dry chicken. Rub both sides of butterflied chicken with dry rub and let sit in covered glass baking dish in the refrigerator for up to 8 hours. Before cooking, brush off excess rub, then place in water smoker, skin side up, and brush with baste. (For a more flavorful smoke, mix apple, cherry, peach or pear wood with oak for smoke.) Cook at 200°F for $3\frac{1}{2}$ hours, moistening with basting mix every half hour. When done, wrap in foil, pour in remaining baste and seal tightly, setting on counter to seal in juices and absorb sauce. Cut chicken into quarters using poultry shears and serve. *Serves 4-6.*

When cooking big birds, wrap the parts in aluminum foil at different intervals (wings first, then legs, then breast) to maximize the smoke time on bigger pieces, which can take the heat.

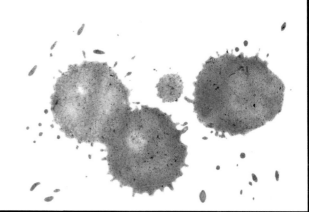

Apple & Onion Smoked Turkey

1 12- to 14-pound turkey

Dry rub:

$\frac{1}{2}$ teaspoon oregano

$\frac{1}{2}$ teaspoon ground sage

$\frac{1}{4}$ teaspoon garlic powder

$\frac{1}{4}$ teaspoon salt

$\frac{1}{4}$ teaspoon freshly ground black pepper

$\frac{1}{4}$ teaspoon ground celery seed

$\frac{1}{4}$ teaspoon poultry seasoning

Stuffing spices/fruit:

1 lemon, cut into quarters

1 apple, cut into quarters

1 orange, cut into quarters

1 onion, cut into quarters

1 bunch fresh rosemary (5 or 6 sprigs)

Basting spray:

$\frac{1}{2}$ cup apple juice

$\frac{1}{2}$ cup white wine

It takes approximately 24 hours to thaw a frozen five-pound chicken in a refrigerator.

Rinse turkey. Remove giblets. Pat-dry. Sprinkle inside of cavity with dry rub. Place quartered fruit and onion and rosemary sprigs inside turkey. Close opening with a dry French roll or thick slice of bread.

Place bird over water pan in smoker. Cook for 4 to 4$\frac{1}{2}$ hours, moistening two or three times during cooking time with basting spray. Use white oak, apple and alder wood (if available). Don't oversmoke; a little bit of smoke over a 4-hour period adds up to a heap o' smoke.

If it's Sunday and you're watching a pro game, don't even look at the turkey until the second half begins. If you're enjoying a baseball game, take the first peek at the seventh-inning stretch. When the internal temperature of the thigh (or thickest part of the bird) reaches 160°F seal bird in foil after final and generous spray of baste liquid. Take off heat and let the turkey rest and reabsorb its juices for 20 to 30 minutes. Have a sip o' cider or a brew and sharpen that carvin' knife. *Serves* 10-12.

Really Wild Turkey

2 cups Wild Turkey bourbon
   (or substitute your favorite hootch)
2 cups whole milk
2 cups orange juice
$\frac{1}{4}$ cup corn oil
$\frac{1}{2}$ teaspoon cayenne pepper
1 10- to 12-pound turkey
1 tablespoon paprika

The night before you plan to cook, mix bourbon, milk, orange juice, corn oil and cayenne pepper. Remove giblets from turkey. If you have a kitchen syringe, inject liquid into the turkey in several places and use remainder as marinade. Otherwise simply store the turkey in a plastic bag with the marinade and refrigerate, turning several times. One hour before cooking, remove turkey from refrigerator and rub down with paprika. Let sit at room temperature. Prepare the smoker for barbecuing at 300°F. Cook 4 to 6 hours or until internal temperature reaches 170°F. Let sit for 30 minutes before carving (bird should continue to cook to 180°F). Serves 8-10.

This one was inspired while watching a TV chef cook turkey with brandy on television. We figured such an American dish deserved a more local libation.

Gobbler Burgers

2 pounds ground turkey
1 medium onion, finely chopped
Paprika
Ground black pepper
Garlic powder
Chopped cilantro
Apple juice

Two hours before cooking, combine turkey and chopped onion in a bowl. Form into 8 patties. Sprinkle with paprika, black pepper, garlic powder, and cilantro to taste. Bring smoker to 250°F. Place burgers on grill away from flame. Cook 1 hour, occasionally spraying with apple juice. Because of health considerations, burgers should be well cooked. Serve on buns with mustard and ketchup or sauce of choice. *Serves* 4-6.

Rich Davis of Kansas City, founder of the KC Masterpiece restaurant chain, reportedly plants two trees for every one used in the restaurants' barbecue pits.

Chicken Fajita-ville

1 tablespoon paprika
2 teaspoons black pepper
1 teaspoon sugar
4 large chicken breasts
2 large green peppers
2 large red peppers
4 large onions
2 tablespoons extra virgin olive oil
8 large tortillas

Mix paprika, pepper and sugar and rub thoroughly into chicken. Refrigerate 3 hours. Slice peppers and onions. Prepare fire (preferably with mesquite) at 250°F. Lay chicken and vegetables on grill, with vegetables as far away from fire as possible. After 30 minutes, turn chicken and remove vegetables. Sauté vegetables in a frying pan in oil until soft. Warm tortillas in oven in aluminum foil. After 30 minutes, remove chicken. Dice chicken and peppers. Chop onions. Serve on tortillas with rice, beans, guacamole and salsa. *Serves* 4.

Wood You Smoke?

The Hardwoods and Fruitwoods of "Q"

Real barbecuing and smoke cooking require hardwoods and fruitwoods. Just as important as choosing the right spices, selecting the proper wood for the food you're cooking can be vital to obtaining perfect results.

Woods, like spices and herbs, have distinct characteristics and flavors, which range from brash to barely there. Following is a list of many of the preferred woods barbecuers around the country use to flavor their cooking:

Alder – Alder is native to the Pacific Northwest and is a mild, sweet wood. Great for balancing out stronger woods like hickory or mesquite. In the Pacific Northwest, they use it for salmon, but it also imparts a nice sweetness to pork.

Apple – By far the most popular of the fruitwoods, apple is neutral and sweet and can be used with anything. Try it on poultry or fish (salmon, trout, sturgeon, shark or swordfish) and you'll be (excuse the expression) hooked.

Cherry – A wonderful, sweet wood that can sometimes darken the meat or poultry you're cooking. Domestic varieties are wonderful and mellow out the flavor of stronger woods.

Grapevines – The rage in California, vines impart a nice flavor to lighter meats, fish and poultry. A few fanatics say cuttings from different varietals impart the flavors of their grapes (Chardonnay vines produce a Chardonnay-flavored smoke, etc.), but that requires a taste sensitivity beyond most people.

Herbs – Many people soak rosemary branches, thyme and basil leaves in water and then throw them on for the last 30 minutes of smoking. From experience, rosemary works the best: Using a bunch of tied-up branches to baste meats on the grill imparts a wonderful rosemary essence.

Hickory – The wood of choice for much of the country. Most hickory sold in stores is a stronger variety than you can get from "natural" resources. Too much hickory can turn food bitter, so apply the smoke in moderation or temper it with cherry, apple or another "mild" wood. It's the only wood to use for smoking hams.

Maple – Try sugar maple for a really sweet smoke, but, as with cherry, it can darken meat (perfect for brisket, though). Mix with alder for a nice "smoke cocktail."

Mesquite – The favored wood of the West. Mesquite is great for brisket b burns too hot and fast for fish and pou try pieces (whole birds are okay). It's very oily wood and can be quite punge if overused. Temper with alder or cher for a nice mix.

Oak – Another standby for barbecuers around the country, oak is often used in a mix with hickory, mesquite or fruitwoods. Burns clean and with moderate heat. Many think red oak is the best, but all varieties can be used with success.

Onion skins – (Also includes garlic skins and cuttings) Soak skins in water for 30 minutes, then put in aluminum foil packages so the skins will smolder, not flame.

Peach – Another sweet wood, peach can lose its "flavor" if kept for a long time after cutting. Use in conjunction with oak or hickory. For superb grilled salmon, try mixing peach with alder.

Plum – Similar to peach, but use only the fruit-bearing varieties. The others can be bitter.

Pecan – Provides a mildly nutty flavor that complements anything you smoke with it. A little goes a long way though, and it can easily be mixed with a fruitwood for a delightful "cocktail."

Wine barrel scrapings – Another California "rage." Taking old, discarded barrels and turning them into chips or chunks (also whiskey barrels) is supposed to produce a nicely flavored smoke, but the jury is still out on this.

Wine chips – Take any old wood chips, chunks or pieces and soak them in a cheap wine for several hours, then use them in fire. Don't use the $49 bottle of Cabernet Sauvignon!

If you're using a gas grill or normal charcoal grill to smoke, try placing the wood on an aluminum pie plate or sheet of heavy-duty aluminum foil, and then place that next to the coals or gas jets. That way the wood won't flame up and will char and smoke more slowly.

Split (Personality) Chicken

1 4- to 5-pound chicken, cut into pieces

Shortening, for frying

Marinade:

4 cups buttermilk

2 tablespoons Jamaican Pickapeppa Sauce

Frying coat:

$1\frac{1}{3}$ cups flour

2 tablespoons bacon bits

$\frac{1}{2}$ teaspoon paprika

$\frac{1}{4}$ teaspoon freshly ground black pepper

$\frac{1}{4}$ teaspoon onion salt

Garnish:

2 tablespoons bacon bits

2 tablespoons dried parsley

Wash and pat-dry chicken. Put chicken in a large plastic bag and cover with half the buttermilk-pepper sauce mixture, reserving the other half in another container. Place in a pan in the refrigerator and chill overnight, turning once or twice. Just before cooking, remove chicken and let stand at room temperature for 30 minutes.

Drain chicken pieces (discard liquid) and cook on smoker grill for 30 to 40 minutes at 220°F over oak-hickory or fruit wood smoke. Remove partially cooked chicken and, using remaining marinade, soak for 15 to 20 minutes in a flat pan.

Put pepper, paprika, onion salt, bacon bits and flour in a large bag. Drain buttermilk from chicken pieces and drop them one at a time into the bag, shaking and coating each piece with flour mixture.

Melt shortening in a large skillet and heat until fat bubbles. Fill pan with chicken pieces, placing pieces skin side down. Cover, reduce heat to medium and fry each side for 10 minutes.

Drain and place chicken on paper towels, then place on heated platter. Sprinkle bacon bits and dried parsley over chicken just before it's served. Crispy and crunchy outside, smoky moist inside. Wowser!!! *Serves 4-6.*

Honey Dijon
Barbecued Chicken

1 3-pound chicken, cut into quarters
$\frac{1}{2}$ cup olive oil
$\frac{1}{2}$ cup white zinfandel
$\frac{1}{4}$ cup clover honey
2 tablespoons Dijon mustard
2 garlic cloves, crushed
1 teaspoon ground black pepper
$\frac{1}{2}$ teaspoon salt

Wash and pat-dry chicken and place in two sealable plastic bags. Pour mixture of oil, wine, honey, mustard, garlic, pepper and salt over chicken. Seal. Marinate in refrigerator for 2 to 4 hours, turning occasionally.

Place remaining marinade in a saucepan and heat to boiling, then let simmer for 5 minutes.

Grill chicken with lid down over medium-hot coals for 20 to 30 minutes per side or until cooked through, basting frequently with the reserved marinade. *Serves* 4.

Carolyn Wells, co-founder,
Kansas City Barbecue Society

Harvey Duckbanger

¾ cup vodka

¼ cup orange juice

2 tablespoons Galliano

1 5-pound duckling

1 teaspoon garlic powder

Cayenne pepper

Mix vodka, orange juice and Galliano in roasting pan. Place duckling in pan and refrigerate for 6 hours. Turn several times and baste in liquid mixture. Dry bird and rub with garlic powder and cayenne pepper. Preheat the grill to 300°F. Cook duck on rack with water-filled drip pan below (ducks are quite fat and will render much fat). Cook for 30 minutes on each side or until cooked to internal temperature of 180°F. *Serves* 4.

Soak wood chips or chunks in wine, beer, fruit juice or your favorite Scotch for at least an hour before using.

Ridgefield Smoked Duck

8 large duck legs

Dry rub:

½ teaspoon dried thyme

½ teaspoon salt

½ teaspoon freshly ground black pepper

Basting spray:

¼ cup cider vinegar

1 tablespoon barbecue sauce

Dash Tabasco Sauce

Trim excess fat from legs. Rub thyme, salt and pepper mixture well into legs and marinate for 1 to 2 hours at room temperature in a covered dish.

Place the legs, skin side down, on smoker grill. Use fruitwoods or alder for smoke. Oak and hickory produce too strong a smoke flavor. Turn legs over after 1 hour.

Cook at 200°F for 2 to 2½ hours until leg bone twists easily. Remove legs from heat and shred meat into a metal or ceramic bowl. Add vinegar, barbecue sauce and Tabasco and mix well.

Serve hot on toasted thinly sliced French or rye bread, lightly spread with garlic butter. *Serves* 4.

"Q" Birdies

4 Cornish game hens, $1\frac{1}{2}$ pounds each

Marinade:

1 cup tequila

1 cup Grand Marnier

$\frac{1}{4}$ cup olive oil

1 large sweet red onion, finely diced

$\frac{1}{4}$ cup cider vinegar

1 teaspoon paprika

$\frac{1}{2}$ teaspoon ground lemon pepper

$\frac{1}{4}$ teaspoon salt

$\frac{1}{4}$ teaspoon freshly ground black pepper

$\frac{1}{4}$ teaspoon garlic salt

Dash Tabasco Sauce

Dash Worcestershire sauce

Wash and pat-dry hens. One day before you wish to barbecue, place birds in a 2-quart, sealable plastic bag. Pour in the marinade ingredients and place bag in the refrigerator. Chill for at least 12 hours, turning as often as convenient.

Before smoking, drain birds and save the marinade for basting. Let birds come to room temperature before putting in smoker. Place, breast side down, on grill and cook for $2\frac{1}{2}$ hours, basting every 20 minutes with the marinade. Turn at least two times during cooking. Birds are ready to serve when internal temperature reaches 180°F and legs move easily. Pierce one thigh with a fork; if the juices are clear, birds are done. Cover with foil and let cooked birds rest for 10 to 15 minutes. Serve whole or cut in half. *Serves* 4.

Meat thermometers take the guesswork out of barbecue, but they tend to become unreadable in a smoky grill. Use the instant-read variety. Keep them outside the oven and stick them in the meat periodically to check doneness. Their small probes do little damage to the meat.

Smok'n Chick'n

1 large chicken (5 pounds or more)

Marinade:

1 cup Italian salad dressing (the zestier the better)

$\frac{1}{2}$ cup spicy barbecue sauce

$\frac{1}{2}$ cup rice wine vinegar

$\frac{1}{2}$ cup apple cider

Dry rub:

$\frac{1}{4}$ teaspoon freshly ground black pepper

$\frac{1}{2}$ teaspoon paprika

$\frac{1}{2}$ teaspoon dried summer savory

$\frac{1}{2}$ teaspoon ground sage

$\frac{1}{4}$ teaspoon onion salt

Basting spray:

Apple juice

Wash and pat-dry chicken. Pour marinade into cavity and over chicken; sprinkle dry ingredients inside and over moistened chicken. Place in a sealable plastic bag. Marinate for at least 4 hours.

Place chicken in smoker and cook at 225°F for 4 hours, turning two or three times. Baste with apple juice several times. When done let bird rest sealed in aluminum foil for at least 20 minutes. Carve and serve with barbecue sauce on the side. *Serves* 4-6.

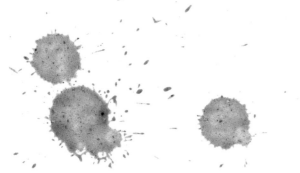

"Q" on the Wing

2 dozen chicken wings

$\frac{1}{4}$ cup lemon juice

$\frac{1}{4}$ cup vegetable oil

1 tablespoon salt

1 teaspoon garlic salt

2 teaspoons onion powder

1 teaspoon chopped cilantro

1 teaspoon paprika

1 teaspoon sugar

$\frac{1}{4}$ teaspoon ground ginger

Clip tips from wings. Mix lemon juice and vegetable oil. Sprinkle on chicken wings. Mix remaining ingredients. Roll chicken wings in resulting blend and refrigerate at least 4 hours. Cook wings until crisp. *Serves* 4-6.

Yellow Bird

1 4- to 5-pound chicken, cut into pieces

$\frac{1}{4}$ cup lemon juice

$\frac{1}{4}$ cup corn oil

1 teaspoon mustard seeds

1 teaspoon onion powder

Mix lemon juice, corn oil, mustard seeds, and onion powder. Turn chicken pieces in paste and place in a sealable plastic bag for 4 hours. Prepare grill to 250°F. Place chicken on grill and cook for 1 hour, turning often. *Serves* 4.

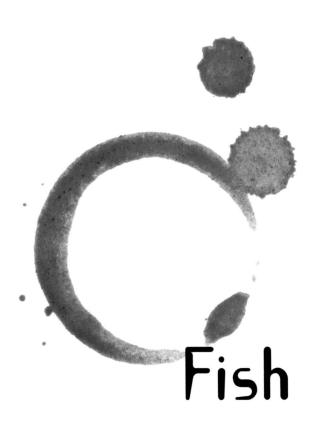

Fish

The Shell Game

2 dozen clams or mussels
1 tablespoon cornstarch
1 stick butter
Juice of 1 large lemon

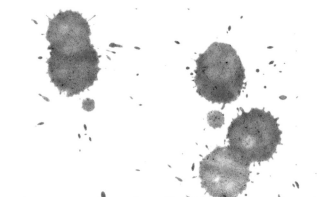

Scrub clams or mussels, cutting off any beard and discarding shellfish that are partially open. Mix cornstarch into a large pot of cold water. Place the clams or mussels in water-cornstarch mixture for 45 minutes. As they sit in the mixture, they will purify themselves. Prepare grill to high heat. When the clams or mussles are ready to come out of water-cornstarch mixture, rinse under fresh water. Place on grill and cover. Melt butter and stir in lemon juice. The clams or mussels will begin to cook in their own liquid and open in 5 to 10 minutes (check regularly). As they open (do not overcook), remove with tongs (the shells will be quite hot). Discard any that don't fully open. Remove meat with cocktail forks and dip in drawn butter or your favorite light barbecue sauce. Eat immediately if you are serving as snacks around the grill. If you are serving at the table, transfer open shellfish to container and keep in warm oven until ready to serve.

Clams and mussels aren't typically thought of as barbecue food, but if you think about it, an argument could be made that the clambakes of New England were some of the country's earliest "Q" events: the local bounty cooking over wood fires. At any rate, they make easy and quick grilling for those occasions when you don't have time to cook for the long haul. They also make great fill-in food when you're standing around the grill waiting for your big cut to finish. Clams and mussels adapt well to gas grill cooking as they cook quickly at fairly high temperatures. *Serves* 4.

One of the most treasured accolades in the "Q" world is the designation Ph.B. This Doctorate of Barbecue is sparingly awarded for "outstanding contributions to barbecue" by Remus Powers (the Dean of Greasehouse University) and the Kansas City Barbecue Society.

Jerry's Grilled Willapa Oysters

2 to 3 dozen large oysters

Marinade:

$\frac{1}{2}$ cup melted butter or margarine

$\frac{1}{2}$ cup white wine

$\frac{1}{4}$ cup sweet barbecue sauce

2 tablespoons lemon juice

1 tablespoon chopped garlic

1 tablespoon chopped fresh parsley

Dash Tabasco Sauce

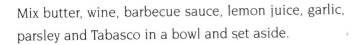

Mix butter, wine, barbecue sauce, lemon juice, garlic, parsley and Tabasco in a bowl and set aside.

Place unshucked oysters on a very hot grill and heat until oysters open. Using heat-proof barbecue gloves, carefully remove top shell and place oysters back on grill.

Drizzle marinade onto each oyster and close top of grill. Heat 4 to 5 minutes and serve hot from the grill. Have plenty of bread available to soak up oyster juice-sauce mixture. Good with wine, beer or Jack Daniel's (taken neat only). *Serves 4.*

As a special treat, two of the photographers at The Columbian invited me to dinner—a special dinner featuring seven dozen Willapa Bay oysters. They couldn't cook them quickly enough for their two guests and we all downed the shelled delicacies as fast as they came off the grill. Fresh, fresh oysters are the secret here.

Salmon Steaks à la Roger

4 large 1½-inch-thick salmon steaks

Marinade:

½ cup packed light brown sugar

¼ cup butter or margarine

¼ cup honey

¼ cup mango juice

1 tablespoon brandy

Dash crushed red pepper

Flavored butter:

2 tablespoons mashed mango

¼ teaspoon ground white pepper

¼ teaspoon dried dill

½ cup butter, softened

Combine marinade ingredients and cook in a saucepan for 4 to 5 minutes over low heat. Place salmon in glass baking dish and pour cooled marinade over steaks. Turn often as you marinate for 1 hour.

While fish is grilling, mix mashed mango, white pepper and dill with softened butter and set aside.

Brush off excess marinade and reserve to baste steaks during cooking. Grill over hot coals for approximately 12 minutes per side. Serve with 1 teaspoon of mango butter on the side or on top of steaks. *Serves 4.*

Salmon Martini

¼ cup fresh dill sprigs

1 teaspoon rock salt

1 teaspoon cracked black pepper

1 butterflied salmon (minus head and tail)

2 cups gin or vodka

½ cup dry vermouth (less for dry martini enthusiasts)

¼ cup olive oil

2 teaspoons dried thyme

1 bay leaf

2 teaspoons onion powder

2 teaspoons rock salt

Juice of 1 large lemon

Mix dill, salt and pepper and rub into exposed surface of fish. Place fish, covered, in refrigerator for 2 hours. Mix alcohol, vermouth, oil, thyme, bay leaf, onion powder, salt and lemon juice (shaking or stirring according to your mixological philosophy). Pour over fish and return to refrigerator for 3 hours. Prepare grill at 300°F using alder wood, if available. Reserve marinade and warm in saucepan. Let salmon stand at room temperature for 30 minutes before cooking. Place salmon, exposed side down, on foil away from fire for 35 minutes. Turn and mop with reserved liquid. Cook for 35 minutes or until done.

High-octane cocktails are mercifully back in vogue and it seems only right to treat the condemned salmon to a final martini before putting it on the grill. *Serves 4-6.*

Lemon Grilled Catfish

½ cup unsalted butter, softened
1 garlic clove, crushed
6 catfish fillets, about 5 to 7 ounces each
2 tablespoons lemon pepper

Combine butter and garlic in a bowl; mix well. Coat both sides of fillets lightly with some of the butter mixture; sprinkle with lemon pepper. Place fillets on grill rack in covered grill. Grill over medium-hot coals for 6 to 7 minutes. Turn and baste with remaining butter mixture. Grill for 5 minutes more or until fish flakes easily. Serve with barbecue or fruit salsa. *Serves 6.*

Carolyn Wells, Kansas City
Carolyn is the "Godmother" of barbecue and of this book, and a true and dear friend.

Over the Rainbows

4 large $1\frac{1}{2}$- to 2-pound rainbow trout
   (fresh, if possible), cleaned
$\frac{1}{4}$ cup melted butter or margarine
1 tablespoon lime juice concentrate
$\frac{1}{4}$ cup finely crushed Kaffir lime leaves
$\frac{1}{4}$ cup packed light brown sugar
1 tablespoon freshly ground black pepper
$\frac{1}{2}$ teaspoon garlic salt

Cheesecloth soak:
$\frac{1}{2}$ cup olive oil
$\frac{1}{4}$ cup lime juice concentrate
1 tablespoon salt

Combine butter and lime juice concentrate and brush trout inside with this mixture. Roll in a mixture of lime leaves, sugar, pepper and salt, coating well. Tightly wrap each fish in cheesecloth and refrigerate overnight. Before smoking, bring fish to room temperature by setting on counter for 30 minutes.

Place whole wrapped fish in glass baking dish and pour the soak over each fish; let cheesecloth absorb the liquid. Place fish on grill and cook 40 to 50 minutes in 200°F smoker. If you can use alder, lime or lemon wood for smoke flavor, the results will be incredible. Otherwise, use a very light oak wood for approximately half the cooking time. DO NOT USE HICKORY.

Serve on a platter with fish still wrapped in cheesecloth. Cut them open at tableside for dramatic effect. *Serves* 4.

One really serious approach to "Q" utensils we've seen is one of those large tool chests on castors that car mechanics use. They lock up tight, can stow just about anything and move easily from garage to patio as the seasons change.

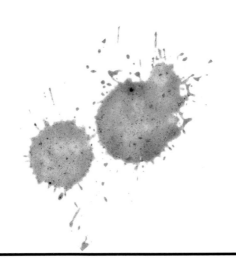

Dave's World Famous BBQ Basting Sauce

2 sticks (1 cup) butter
$\frac{1}{3}$ cup lemon juice
$1\frac{1}{2}$ teaspoons soy sauce
$1\frac{1}{2}$ teaspoons Worcestershire sauce
1 tablespoon chopped fresh parsley
1 teaspoon sweet basil
$\frac{1}{2}$ teaspoon garlic powder
Salt and pepper to taste

Melt the butter and add the remaining ingredients. Use to baste salmon, albacore or other firm fish while cooking. *Makes about $1\frac{1}{3}$ cups.*

Before grilling or smoking, use a nonstick cooking spray to coat the grill itself and the inside lid of the smoker or grill. Makes cleanup easier and food won't stick.

BQ Albacore

4 albacore tuna steaks, about $\frac{1}{2}$ to
$\frac{3}{4}$ inch thick
8 strips bacon
2 cups soy sauce
1 tablespoon lemon juice
2 garlic cloves, finely chopped
Dash Tabasco Sauce
Salt and pepper to taste

Wrap each albacore steak with 2 pieces of bacon and secure with a toothpick. Put steaks in a glass baking dish and marinate overnight in the soy sauce, lemon, garlic, Tabasco, salt and pepper mixture to which enough water has been added to cover fish. One hour before you wish to barbecue, let fish come to room temperature.

Barbecue off heat, adding hickory, alder or fruit wood chips to briquette side of barbecue. Cook 4 to 6 minutes per side until fish is done but still moist. *Serves* 4.

Cat Talbot, captain
Fishing Vessel Millie C,
Mendocino, California

Char-Broiled King Salmon Fillets

2 pounds fresh king salmon fillets
10 tablespoons unsalted butter, softened
3 tablespoons lime juice
1 shot tequila (use Cuervo for best taste)
1 ripe avocado
2 tablespoons chopped cilantro
2 tablespoons water
1 tablespoon olive oil
1 teaspoon chopped garlic
1 teaspoon chopped shallots
3 tablespoons chicken stock
Salt and pepper to taste

Smoking should be done at between 200°F to 220°F. If the temperature gets too high, close the dampers. If temperature is too low, open them and add more soaked wood chips or wood chunks.

Prepare the barbecue grill. Cut the fillet into four portions, discarding bones. Cover and refrigerate. In a food processor, combine the butter, 1 tablespoon lime juice, and tequila. Process until smooth and set aside. In a bowl, mash the avocado with 1 tablespoon cilantro and the water; add salt to taste and set aside.

To prepare the sauce, heat a sauté pan, add the olive oil, and lightly sauté the garlic and shallots. Add the remaining 2 tablespoons lime juice, the mashed avocado, and the chicken stock; salt and pepper to taste and bring to a gentle boil.

When grill is hot, coat the salmon fillets with the tequila butter, salt and pepper, and grill on each side for 3 minutes per side. Transfer to a warm serving platter. Add the remaining 1 tablespoon of cilantro to the sauce, pour over the salmon, and serve. *Serves* 4.

White Tie and Lobster Tails

1 stick butter, or as much as needed
1 teaspoon thyme
Juice of 1 lemon
Salt and pepper to taste
1 lobster per person

Melt butter and mix with thyme, lemon juice, salt and pepper. Keep over low heat. Plunge lobsters in large kettle of vigorously boiling water. When water comes to a second boil, remove now-dead lobsters with tongs, being very careful not to scald yourself. Wrap in towels to protect yourself from burning and snap off tails. Replace remainder of lobsters (or just the claws, if you don't like body meat) in boiling water and boil as you normally would lobster. With a stout knife, split lobster tail from end to end, cutting through soft underside first. Brush exposed meat with butter mixture. Place, shell side down, on grill over medium heat. Brush again in 20 minutes and turn over for 5 to 10 minutes. Serve with tails and bodies, using remainder of butter mixture for dipping.

As a New Englander, I used to be a snob about lobsters, saying: "Water is the only cooking medium for these noble warriors of the deep, and you mustn't ever smoke them." I had to travel to Hawaii, where I sampled the large, clawless variety, to get my head turned around on that one. I still believe that smoking the tender claws is overkill and shouldn't be done, but don't let anyone tell you the tails can't benefit from a whiff of smoke. If you're worried that lobsters are too expensive and highfalutin for your "Q" cronies, consider this: It has only been relatively recently that these crustaceans were considered the domain of the tuxedo crowd (mainly due to escalating prices). You only need to wrestle with shelling one of these babies to be disabused of the notion that they are for dainty company. Besides, when New England was first settled, lobsters were so plentiful that they were regularly served to prisoners in colonial jails.

A BBQ FIT FOR A KING

The World's Largest Salmon Barbecue

Once a year for the past 27 years, the tiny coastal village of Fort Bragg, California, has gleefully played host to one of America's most unique barbecue festivals.

It's a gathering of thousands—where almost half the guests literally give up their lives to attend.

You see, being invited to dinner here, for the piscine set anyway, means you ARE dinner. An invitation to attend is terminal for royalty. Kings, as in king salmon, are dying to attend. Filleted, drizzled with lemon butter, and—perish the thought—grilled. A salmon's worst nightmare come true. A sacrificial burnt offering, as it were.

But, as often is the way in Mother Nature's realm, the hundreds of fish that make the ultimate sacrifice do so, albeit unwillingly, so that many more of their kind *may live*.

The festival is not a cooking contest but rather a huge Saturday-nearest-the-Fourth-of-July picnic, which is held in a colorful shoreline park overlooking one of the West Coast's most scenic marinas. Grills churn out clouds of fragrant smoke that drift over long rows of bobbing fishing boats, the very same fishing boats that brought the honored guests to this, their ultimate party. The barbecue

is also a benefit for the local Salmon Restoration Association, providing the primary funding for two local fish hatcheries and their efforts to replenish the once-great numbers of salmon that formerly flourished in northern California waters.

Thousands of king salmon, pulled from the fertile waters off the spectacular Fort Bragg-Mendocino coast by local fishermen (and fisherwomen) are THE featured course in what has been billed as "The World's Largest Salmon BBQ."

More than 200 volunteers garnered from the ranks of local associations spend the day preparing upward of 5,000 pounds of the succulent fish. Marinating huge steaks and fillets in olive oil, lemon, parsley and garlic, grilling the fish on several dozen large charcoal grills, and then tenderly serving up the piping hot salmon onto the plates of 5,000 paying guests. Yup, you did the math. 5,000 pounds—5,000 people. That's no quarter-pounder! Overgenerous portions aside, this seafood event is so popular that it draws attendees from as far as 200 miles away who brave the challengingly curlicued two-lane road that winds up the dramatic coastline from San Francisco to the quaint seaside village of Fort Bragg.

"I can't believe how big the portions are," gushed Maryanne Gomes, who watched her son, Oliver, inhale a quarter of a salmon, "there's enough here to feed three people! A friend of mine told me about this and I didn't believe him, but I drove up here from Santa Cruz anyway."

Santa Cruz, by the way, is 179 miles to the south—not a bad drive for lunch!

American flags and tri-colored bunting wave gently in ocean breezes that easily cool even the hottest July temperatures. Sea gulls wheel conspiratorially and expectantly overhead, the smell of the nearby crashing surf competing with the fragrant smoke pouring from row after row of fiery grills. Amid the oohs and aahs of ravenous diners, who endured long lines queuing up to two hours before the festival officially opened, enthusiastic bands serenade the jammed picnic tables with everything from hard rock to soft put-your-hand-over-your-heart patriotic ditties. Norman Rockwell (or perhaps Arthur Fiedler) surely is hiding somewhere in the crowd, plate balanced in one hand, chilled flagon of rosé wine in the other.

The salmon just show up and aren't supposed to do much. After all, they are the main guests. Burp!

Patrons are served gargantuan portions of orange-hued fish dripping with butter, olive oil and spices. Each platter is piled high with almost a full pound of tender fish, barbecued corn on the cob, a mountainous mound of green salad, and "as many pieces as you wish, sir" hot-off-the-grill garlic bread. Chilled California wines and beer wet cultured and uncultured whistles, alike.

Various Fort Bragg associations divide the labor for the day: the Lions uncork and pour beer and wine, the Soroptimists butter and grill a thousand loaves of oh-so-gar-licky bread, the Rotarians shuck 5,000 ears of corn, athletic members of the Club Latino Americano toss a half-ton of salad, and the Knights of Columbus ladle out gallons of java and punch. All the while, the charming Noyo Women for Fisheries handle ticket sales and generally act as spir-ited hostesses.

The salmon just show up and aren't supposed to do much. After all, they are the main guests. Burp!

For further information on efforts to restore this valuable resource, please contact the Salmon Restoration Association of California, Inc., P. O. Box 1448, Fort Bragg, CA 95437. The Not Just A Cookbook—a cookbook featuring an extensive collection of seafood recipes—can be purchased from the Noyo Women for Fisheries, P. O. Box 137, Fort Bragg, CA 95437. Proceeds from the sale of this cookbook go into a scholarship fund for Fort Bragg-Mendocino graduating high school seniors who are connected with the fishing industry.

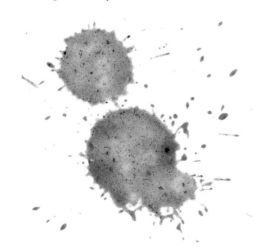

Dodie's Salmon Cream Sauce

2 cups whipping cream
2 egg yolks
$2\frac{1}{2}$ tablespoons mustard
$2\frac{1}{2}$ tablespoons flour
$\frac{1}{2}$ cup soft margarine
$\frac{1}{2}$ small onion, chopped
Juice of 1 lemon
Pinch tarragon
Pinch parsley

Blend ingredients in a bowl with a wire whisk, or in a blender. Place in a saucepan and cook over low heat until mixture thickens. Serve with salmon fillets or steaks. *Makes about $2\frac{1}{2}$ cups.*

Dodie Scott
Fishing Vessel Sabrina, Fort Bragg, California

New Yorkers used to barbecue turtles in the early 18th century.

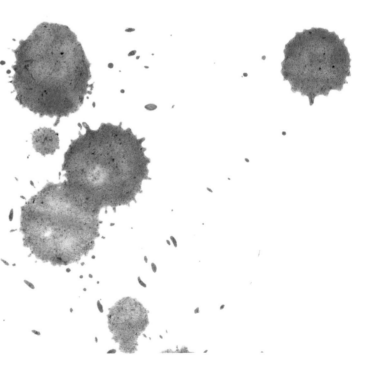

Rum Soused BBQ Shrimps

2 pounds medium shrimp (about 32)

Lime and mango ratatouille:

3 ripe mangos

1 green pepper

1 small sweet red onion

1 cup pineapple juice

$\frac{1}{4}$ cup lime juice

3 tablespoons balsamic vinegar

1 tablespoon chopped fresh basil

Freshly ground black pepper and salt to taste

Marinade:

$1\frac{1}{2}$ cups pineapple juice

$\frac{1}{2}$ cup light or dark rum

6 tablespoons fresh lime juice (4 limes)

2 tablespoons chopped fresh parsley

2 garlic cloves, minced

$\frac{1}{2}$ teaspoon sea salt

$\frac{1}{2}$ teaspoon freshly ground black pepper

Peel and finely dice mangos, carefully cutting fruit away from large pit. Seed and finely dice green pepper. Finely dice red onion. Mix fruit-vegetable mixture with liquid ingredients. Add chopped basil and pepper and salt, and stir. Set aside.

Combine marinade ingredients in a large bowl, add shrimp and refrigerate for 2 to 3 hours only. (More time than that will allow the citric acid in the marinade to begin to "cook" the shrimp.) Drain shrimp and put on grill in smoker (preheated to 200°F) for 15 to 20 minutes until they are just cooked through. Test one to see if it's done. Remove from grill and chill for several hours. Serve with the bowl of lime and mango ratatouille for dipping shrimp. *Serves* 4-6.

If you don't have an expensive thermometer on your rig, a candy thermometer mounted in a hole in the lid will do the trick. They measure in about the right heat range you will cook in and have a probe long enough to monitor the middle of the grill. In a pinch, put your palm over the grill top. If you can hold it there for five seconds, the fire is low enough for real barbecue.

On any given weekend in America, there's a barbecue contest somewhere.

Last year, more than 6 million people attended more than 500 barbecue contests.

Beef

Barbecued Brisket of Beef

1 10- to 12-pound beef brisket
(packer trimmed)

Brisket rub:

$\frac{1}{2}$ cup paprika

$\frac{1}{4}$ cup black pepper

$\frac{1}{4}$ cup salt

$\frac{1}{4}$ cup turbinado sugar

3 tablespoons garlic powder

2 tablespoons chili powder

1 tablespoon onion powder

1 tablespoon dry mustard

1 tablespoon celery salt

$\frac{1}{2}$ teaspoon red pepper

Brisket spray:

1 cup apple cider vinegar

$\frac{1}{2}$ cup beer

1 tablespoon Worcestershire sauce

1 tablespoon olive oil

Fill flour or corn tortillas or gorditas with chopped BBQ pork shoulder or brisket for a tasty luncheon treat.

Combine rub ingredients and massage into brisket. Seal in a plastic bag and refrigerate overnight. Before you barbecue, remove brisket from refrigerator and let it sit at room temperature for 1 hour. Prepare water smoker and bring temperature to 220°F. Fill water pan with water and 16 ounces of beer. Cut one orange and one lemon into thin slices and float in pan.

Place brisket in center of grill over water pan, fat side up, and cook until done. Brisket will shrink dramatically and turn almost totally black. Cook 1 to $1\frac{1}{4}$ hours per pound, a minimum of 12 hours, basting every hour with spray bottle of vinegar, beer, Worcestershire sauce and olive oil mixture.

When cooked, remove meat from grill, spray one more time and seal in aluminum foil. Slice across the grain and serve with a favorite barbecue sauce on the side. *Serves* 12-16.

Rattlesnake Prime Rib

1 10- to 12-pound standing rib roast, preferably prime

Rib rub:

$\frac{1}{2}$ cup olive oil

$\frac{1}{4}$ cup coarsely ground black pepper

$\frac{1}{4}$ cup salt

$\frac{1}{4}$ cup garlic powder

$\frac{1}{4}$ cup brown sugar

1 teaspoon crushed red pepper

Steaming liquid:

2 cups red wine

4 cups water

4 rosemary sprigs

10 fresh basil leaves

Prime rib spray:

$\frac{1}{2}$ cup red wine vinegar

$\frac{1}{2}$ cup red wine

$\frac{1}{4}$ cup olive oil

2 teaspoons honey

Rub roast with olive oil, massaging it into the meat. Rub black pepper, salt, garlic powder, brown sugar and red pepper mixture into meat, coating all sides evenly. Cover tightly and refrigerate overnight. Before cooking, let meat stand at room temperature for 30 to 40 minutes. Heat water smoker to 220°F. Pour red wine into water pan with water. Float rosemary sprigs and fresh basil leaves in water. Place meat, fat side up, in center of grill and cook for $2\frac{1}{2}$ to 3 hours over oak, hickory or fruit woods. Spray every 30 minutes with rib spray. When internal temperature reaches 140°F, remove roast from smoker, seal in foil and let rest for 10 to 15 minutes. Carve and serve immediately. *Serves 8-10.*

Bodacious Brisket

1 4- to 6-pound beef brisket

$\frac{1}{2}$ cup paprika

2 tablespoons brown sugar

2 tablespoons chili pepper

2 tablespoons onion powder

$\frac{1}{4}$ cup yellow mustard

$\frac{1}{2}$ cup beer

$\frac{1}{2}$ cup apple juice

Trim fat from brisket. Mix paprika, sugar, chili pepper and onion powder. Spread mustard on brisket. Coat brisket with prepared rub. Prepare grill at 230°F. Cook brisket over indirect heat for 2 to 4 hours, turning every 30 minutes and spraying with a mixture of beer and apple juice. Brisket is done when internal temperature reaches 150°F. *Serves 6-8.*

A handy new item is the thermometer that has its readout outside the oven. You stick a probe in the meat, and a wire runs out to a digital counter that tells you the temperature without having to lift the grill lid. They even have alarms that tell you when the meat reaches the desired doneness.

Kansas City Strip Steaks

¼ cup Guldens mustard
2 tablespoons lime juice
1 tablespoon brown sugar
1 tablespoon prepared horseradish
2 teaspoons salt
½ teaspoon ground white pepper
4 Kansas City strip steaks, about 1 inch thick
   and 8 ounces each

Mix mustard, lime juice, brown sugar, horseradish, salt and pepper, turning it to a paste. Coat steaks. Marinate in a plastic bag in the refrigerator for 2 hours. Allow to stand at room temperature for 30 minutes. Grill steaks over low heat until done, turning once. *Serves 4.*

On our first trip to Kansas City, we were in a famous steak emporium called the Hereford House and asked what the Kansas City strip steak was on the menu. The waitress described it and we made the mistake of commenting that it sounded pretty much like New York strip steak. "How many steers," she asked, "have you ever seen in New York?" Touché!

Roast Beef

1 cup cooking sherry
1 cup vinegar
1 3-pound boneless rib roast, tied
Vegetable oil
Ground black pepper
Chopped fresh parsley
Dried rubbed sage
Dried rosemary
Dried thyme

The night before you cook, mix sherry and vinegar and pour into a plastic bag. Insert roast and tie shut. Refrigerate, turning occasionally. One hour before grilling, remove roast and pat-dry. Reserve liquid and boil for basting. Slather on vegetable oil and coat with pepper, parsley, sage, rosemary and thyme to taste. Prepare grill to 250°F. Place beef on grill away from fire with drip pan underneath. Cook for 1½ hours (about 25 minutes per pound), basting regularly. Closely monitor internal temperature with thermometer. Cook to 10 degrees below desired doneness (130°F for rare, 140°F for medium, 150°F for well done). Remove and let stand until roast is done to desired temperature. Reserve drippings in pan for gravy. *Serves 4-6.*

Sonny Bryan's flagship restaurant, The Original, is a nondescript building in a nondescript part of Dallas. Some of Sonny's regular customers include Arnold Swarzenegger, Steven Spielberg, Tom Hanks, George Bush, Sylvester Stallone, Eric Clapton, Larry Hagman, Bruce Willis, Jimmy Buffett and Donald Trump.

Foggy City Meat Loaf

Loaf mop:

1 cup cider vinegar

½ cup hearty red wine

2 garlic cloves, roughly chopped

2 tablespoons olive oil

1 tablespoon dried summer savory

1 tablespoon Worcestershire sauce

Meat loaf:

1 medium onion, minced

1 medium red pepper, minced

½ cup sun-dried tomatoes,
   minced and freshened in warm water

2 tablespoons olive oil

1½ pounds ground beef
   (tri-tip or sirloin)

½ pound ground pork
   (shoulder or tenderloin)

1½ cups crushed Ritz or Waverly crackers

1 egg

¼ cup hearty red wine

3 tablespoons favorite barbecue sauce

1 tablespoon minced garlic

1 teaspoon garlic salt

1 teaspoon lemon pepper

½ teaspoon dried oregano

½ teaspoon dried thyme

½ teaspoon dry mustard

Dash Tabasco Sauce

Mix the loaf mop ingredients together and set aside. Preheat smoker to 220°F.

Sauté onion, red pepper, and sun-dried tomatoes until soft in olive oil in a heavy skillet. Place ground meat in a large bowl and add cooked vegetables and remaining ingredients. Using your hands, thoroughly mix into the meat.

Form meat into a loaf and place in a metal or glass loaf pan. Moisten the loaf with the mop and place in center of grill over water pan.

Cook for 1 hour without opening smoker. Then remove pan and remove meat in loaf shape and return to grill. Cook an additional 1½ hours, mopping with liquid every 30 minutes. Ten minutes before you remove meat from heat, brush barbecue sauce or ketchup or a can of undiluted tomato soup on top of meat loaf.

Remove from grill, seal in foil and let meat rest for 10 to 15 minutes before serving. Slice in 1-inch-thick portions. Garnish with fresh parsley and serve a favorite barbecue sauce on the side. *Serves 4-6.*

Transplanted London Broil

$\frac{1}{4}$ cup bourbon
1 London broil, about 2 pounds
Sugar
Salt
Ground black pepper
Mrs. Dash with garlic seasoning blend

Pour bourbon (flavor-rich small-batch brand, if you can afford it) into a small nonreactive pan. Place steak in pan and set in the refrigerator for 2 hours, turning frequently. Coat steak with sugar, salt, pepper and seasoning blend in that order. Reserve liquid for basting. Return steak to refrigerator for 1 hour. Prepare grill to 250°F. Place steak on high grill. Turn steak twice. Rotate twice. Cook 40 minutes or until done. *Serves 6.*

We think the inexpensive and unheralded London broil makes a great cut if you're planning to smoke steak. We've given it a drink of bourbon—America's true quaff—to make the transatlantic voyage a little easier.

Real Fajitas

1 tablespoon paprika

2 teaspoons freshly ground
   black pepper

1 teaspoon Tabasco Sauce

1 teaspoon sugar

2 pounds skirt steak, trimmed

2 large green peppers

2 large red peppers

4 large onions

6 ounces pale ale

8 large tortillas

Mix paprika, pepper, Tabasco sauce and sugar and rub thoroughly into steak. Refrigerate for 3 hours. Slice peppers and onions. Prepare fire (preferably with mesquite) at 250°F. Lay beef and vegetables on grill, with vegetables as far away as possible from fire. After 30 minutes, turn beef and baste with ale. Remove vegetables. Sauté vegetables in oil until soft. Warm tortillas in the oven in aluminum foil. After 30 minutes, baste beef again and move over fire for searing. Drink remaining ale. Dice beef and peppers. Chop onions. Serve on tortillas with rice, refried beans, guacamole, and your favorite salsa. *Serves* 4.

While fajitas are now considered on menus across the country to be anything served with grilled vegetables in a tortilla, the word actually refers to a cut of steak. In Mexico, the skirt steak was slow-cooked to allow all of its flavor to express itself and then served in a taco. When the fajita became popular, the term was misconstrued to be the presentation and not the meat.

IncrEDIBLE Burgers

2 pounds ground beef

Beef seasoning:

3 tablespoons minced red onion

1 teaspoon garlic salt

1 teaspoon lemon pepper

1 tablespoon favorite barbecue sauce

1 egg, lightly beaten

1 tablespoon ginger ale

Steaming liquid:

16 ounces of your favorite beer

4 cups water

Burger spray:

1 cup apple cider

2 tablespoons balsamic vinegar

2 tablespoons olive oil

Mix meat and seasoning ingredients in a large bowl. Form into 8 patties, cover with plastic wrap and refrigerate for 1 hour. Remove meat from refrigerator and let it come to room temperature (approximately 20 minutes).

Preheat smoker to 220°F and pour beer and water into water tray. Add cuttings and skins from onions to the water. Place burgers on oiled grill. Cook burgers for 50 minutes, occasionally spraying with apple cider mixture. *Serves* 8.

Buzz's Barbecue Burgers

2 pounds fatty ground beef

1 medium onion, finely chopped

Paprika

Freshly ground black pepper

Garlic powder

Chopped cilantro

Ground cumin

Apple juice

Two hours before cooking, combine ground beef and onion in a bowl. Form into 8 patties. Sprinkle with paprika, black pepper, garlic powder, cilantro and cumin to taste. Bring smoker to 250°F. Place burgers on grill away from flame. Cook for 40 minutes or until cooked to desired doneness, occasionally spraying with apple juice. If cheeseburgers are desired, melt cheddar cheese over burgers 5 minutes before removing from grill. Serve on buns with mustard and ketchup or sauce of choice. *Serves* 4-6.

Some exotic woods to burn for flavorful smoke: lilac, seaweed, grape vines, fresh herbs (rosemary twigs), pieces of old wine or whiskey barrels.

Irish BBQ
Flanque Steaque

¾ cup unsweetened applesauce

½ cup soy sauce

2 jiggers Bushmill's Irish whiskey, or to taste

3 tablespoons cider vinegar

5 garlic cloves

3 tablespoons chopped green onion

2 pounds flank steak

Spice Islands Beau Monde Seasoning
   (only while grilling the steak)

Mix applesauce, soy sauce, whiskey, vinegar, garlic and onion in a bowl. Puncture the meat all over with a fork and then place the steak in a plastic zip-lock bag and pour in the marinade. Leave meat in the refrigerator overnight, turning the bag occasionally.

Remove the flank steak from the marinade, scraping excess from the meat. Place the marinade in a medium pot and bring to a boil, continue heating until liquid is reduced by one-third.

Cook flank steak over hot coals until rare to medium rare. Slice the steak across the grain into thin strips. Arrange meat on plate and pour the reduced marinade sauce over the steak strips. *Serves 4-6.*

Skirt steaks, the diaphragm muscle of beef cattle, used to be called butcher steaks because they could hardly give them away. Now they sell well as the main ingredient in steak fajitas.

Flank Steak

1 flank steak, about 1½ pounds
1 cup Worcestershire sauce
¼ cup Tennessee whiskey
2 garlic cloves, minced
Olive oil
Freshly ground black pepper

The night before you grill, slightly score flank steak in a crisscross pattern on either side. Combine Worcestershire sauce, whiskey and garlic and pour over steak. Marinate in the refrigerator overnight, turning several times. Leave at room temperature for 1 hour before grilling. Prepare grill to high heat. Coat steak in olive oil. Grill steak quickly (3 to 5 minutes each side). Slice across grain into thin strips immediately after removing from grill. Pepper to taste. *Serves 6-8.*

Buffalo Steaks

¾ cup Italian salad dressing (the zestier the better)

2 tablespoons prepared salsa

1 tablespoon sugar

4 buffalo steaks, about 1 inch thick and 8 ounces each

Salt and pepper to taste

At least 4 hours before cooking, combine dressing, salsa and sugar. Thoroughly slather steaks with marinade in a shallow non-reactive pan. Cover and refrigerate. Reserve excess for mopping. Prepare grill to low heat. Smoke for 1 hour or until meat reaches desired temperature (140°F for rare, 160°F for well done). Mop occasionally with remaining marinade. *Serves* 4.

Canadian entrepreneur Vern Jackson took to the barbecue circuit trying to drum up interest in smokin' with bison (American buffalo), which, he is fond of saying, "tastes like beef wishes it did." Low in cholesterol and fat, it may be a good choice for health-conscious carnivores. This is one way of cooking it.

Brisket Chili

1 4-pound beef brisket

Brisket rub (*page* 107)

1 cup chopped onions

2 garlic cloves, minced

1 green pepper, chopped

1½ tablespoons chili powder

1 teaspoon ground oregano

¾ teaspoon ground cumin

1 16-ounce can crushed tomatoes

1 16-ounce can kidney beans

½ teaspoon Tabasco Sauce

½ teaspoon black pepper

Prepare brisket as Bodacious Brisket (*page* 107). Slice one quarter of meat into bite-size chunks. Serve remainder of beef immediately. In a large saucepan, place brisket chunks with onion, garlic and green pepper and cook over medium heat until soft. Add chili powder, cumin and oregano and cook for 3 minutes. Add tomatoes, kidney beans, Tabasco and black pepper. Cook over low heat for 4 hours. *Serves* 4.

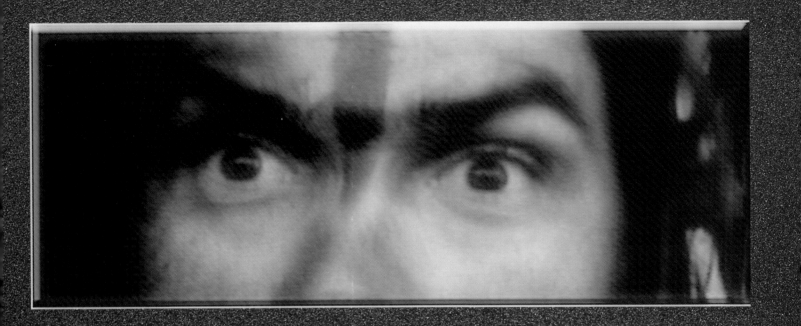

LIKE BEEF?

YOUR ANCESTORS DID.

ANY GRILL CAN COOK A STEAK
BUT CAN IT COOK A PANCAKE?

The Big Easy™ can. With three separate cooking systems, it can cook breakfast, lunch and dinner. So you're not only the keeper of the grill, you're the keeper of the griddle, the deep dish and the smoker. With the Big Easy, you're the ultimate keeper of the flame. For the location of a Big Easy dealer near you visit www.charbroil.com.

Charbroil® is a registered trademark of the W.C. Bradley Co. and The Big Easy™ is a trademark of the W.C. Bradley Co.

Char-Broil. KEEPERS OF THE FLAME™

In smoked meats, as in poultry and fish, a pink color $\frac{1}{4}$ to $\frac{1}{2}$ inch deep under the outside surface is called a "smoke ring" and is one sign of great barbecue. Some barbecuers cheat by adding nitrates to their rubs, causing an unnatural smoke ring, but the proof is in the taste.

A Day in the Life in Brisket Country

Cooking Hunks of Cow

Four A.M. outside the Knights of Columbus hall in Arlington, Texas, on a rainy November Saturday. An alarm wakes Jim Griffin from a sound slumber. The wiry Texan stumbles out of his camper and makes his way to the Blue Flamingo.

Lifting one of the doors on the hulking electric-blue smoker that sits on four wheels not 10 feet from his camper, he glimpses the half-dozen or so 10-pound briskets that have been bathing in smoke since midnight.

Perfect! They're ready for Stage II.

Tearing sheets of tinfoil off a roll, he begins the process of wrapping the huge hunks of cow into shiny gift packages of meat—hidden four or five layers deep in aluminum. The beef insulated and back in the grill, he stokes the fire and watches as the thermometers that monitor the inside of the grill slowly climb from 220°F to as much as 300°F.

He takes one last look at the grill, its Stars & Strips, Stars & Bars and Blue Flamingo flags waving at the stern. Satisfied that all is well with his rig, he crawls back into bed beside his wife, Billie.

Six A.M. on Inwood Road in Dallas. Michael LeMaster is

Beef 123

arriving for work at Sonny Bryan's Restaurant. Michael is the grill-master at the flagship restaurant, The Original, kept just as it was when Sonny was alive and before there were 10 other restaurants of the same name scattered around the metropolitan area. Part of his job is to make sure the two-room brisket shack stays true to its roots, even as the other barbecues in the chain grow bigger and shinier. Man, he even caught hell when he went to move the pile of logs—grill fuel— outside the front window that was blocking the policemen's view into the storefront at night when they cruised by checking for intruders. This is a job for a purist.

Michael relieves the grill guy who has been watching the fire and the hundreds of pounds of meat all night. He walks through the cramped quarters and overlooks his preserve. For LeMaster, this is the culmination of a childhood spent in this north Dallas neigh-borhood and a career spent in the food industry.

As a kid, he went with his parents to Sonny Bryan's as soon as he was old enough to teethe on the bones of their spareribs. He remembers piling into the family car and coming down here when eating out was a major event, a special treat. As a grownup, he worked in the restaurant business before taking a position at one of Sonny's other restaurants. Then, a couple of years ago, management came to him and asked him to be the grillmaster at the flagship.

"I couldn't turn it down," he says. "It meant coming full circle. I'd grown up here. Then I learned about barbecue by playing in the back yard with a barrel. If it was bigger than a bullfrog and smaller than a water buffalo, I'd cook it. And here they were, offering me a chance to work at Sonny's." Now, Michael LeMaster is back where it all started, and a smile crosses his mustached face as he prepares to sell the 500 pounds of beef brisket that have been smoking in his grill overnight.

Seven-thirty A.M., the VFW post in Grand Prairie. Dennis Keuter is just getting started. He arrives in the parking lot with 14 nine-pound briskets, each rubbed down with a mixture of chili powder, lemon pepper, sage, fajita mix, maybe even some SHAKE'N BAKE and some other things. He's not sure what. He's not sure of the proportions, either. He's not one of these go-by-the-recipe guys. It changes every time, depending on what's around and how the mood strikes him. He does know there is no sugar in the mix.

After taking a couple of trips to drag the meat out to a concrete slab next to the clubhouse, he sets to work building a fire in the post's rig, which sits under a sheet-metal awning. On the grill, a plaque reads, "Grill Donated by Bubba and Barbara Witherspoon." Bubba, another vet, built the barbecue himself, using the sleeves they mold concrete columns in and painstakingly putting the whole thing together with a 110-volt wire welder.

Satisfied that everything is right with Bubba's creation, Dennis sets his 14 briskets on the grill and retreats to the warmth of the clubhouse.

Eight A.M., back at the Knights of Columbus. Jim Griffin returns to the Blue Flamingo and gingerly removes his briskets from the grill. They've been in for eight hours, four in foil, four without. Jim's been in Arlington since 4 p.m. the day before. He got off work early in Wichita Falls, Texas, and hauled the whole mess over here in time to make the meat turn-in for the Lone Star Barbecue Association's state championship (or at least it will be a state championship once they get the sanctioning from the

Tearing sheets of tinfoil off a roll, he begins the process of wrapping the huge hunks of cow into shiny gift packages of meat—hidden four or five layers deep in aluminum.

Eleven A.M., the VFW hall. Dennis Keuter has wandered out from the card game going on in a back room to check on his briskets. He's pointing out his babies and indicating their final destinations. "These we'll eat today, these three go to a birthday party on Tuesday." All the pieces of meat have been trimmed to a grilling weight of seven pounds and the extra fat is piled back on top. "That keeps 'em from drying out," Dennis advises.

governor's office). After turn-in, he put marinade and rub on his meat and waited until midnight to start cooking. In the meantime, he caught up with old friends and indulged in the "fellowship" of the "Q" circuit. "Fellowship, not winning, is the object of this," Jim says.

"Barbecue cooking is just a good excuse to drink beer," Billie translates the meaning of the word fellowship for him. "Cookin' ain't got nothing to do with it."

Jim places his brisket into a large cooler and packs it in with newspapers. The meat will stay there for another four hours, still cooking and simmering in its own juices, before he unwraps it and lets it cool until turn-in at the judges tables—his wife's domain.

Billie's a judge. The head judge, Jim hastens to add. She doesn't actually rate the entries, but supervises the whole process. "Otherwise it would look kind of funny if I won."

Glenn Nickolas, one of Griffin's barbecue chums, says the Lone Star grillers "are pretty proud of our system," a double-blind, double-draw method that allows for as many as 20 judges to rate one cooker's meat. The classic Kansas City Barbecue Society system allows for only six judges to try each entry. Nickolas is familiar with that system as he's been up to KC to take their judging course. In fact, he would have been competing at the Jack Daniel's Invitational, another KCBS-sanctioned event, only a few weeks ago, except that he had to have his gall bladder removed.

Glenn explains that the Lone Star rules, which further stipulate that all cuts of meat must be approximately the same size, sliced the same way and in the same number of slices, were modified from the system used by the many chili contests held in Texas.

One of the austerities of the system is the definite lack of barbecue sauce employed at this contest of 23 teams. "In Texas, we don't use sauce," says Glenn. "We believe in meat."

"That's right," adds Jim. "We're turning in product for a meat contest. Not a sauce contest."

Ten A.M. at Sonny Bryan's. Michael LeMaster is rearranging dispensers of barbecue sauce on a hot plate sitting on the condiment counter. LeMaster is one of a few employees who know the recipe, which Sonny's grandfather, Elijah, authored in 1910. The original draft is kept locked in a safe at headquarters. He's not very forthcoming to those who ask for the secrets. He will admit, however, that he cooks with a mixture of oak and hickory smoke. Oak-ry, he calls it.

Soon customers will come pouring in, clamoring for brisket ribs, sausage and chicken—and the sauce to put on them. His shop may be small—seating about 20—but it's where a lot of folks in Dallas come when they want "Q." Even some folks from out of town. Arnold Swarzenegger came sauntering in once with his entourage of 20, and they had to send him to their West End outlet because there wasn't enough space in the dining room, which is lined with elementary-school-style chairs with desktops. Steven Spielberg and Tom Hanks simply had their "Q" delivered to the Mansion Hotel. The list goes on: George Bush, Sylvester Stallone, Eric Clapton, Larry Hagman, Bruce Willis, Jimmy Buffett, Donald Trump, etc., etc. But to LeMaster, the celebrities are "just little extra hits." What really fires his grill is looking out in the parking lot on a sunny day and seeing the locals, the regulars, enjoying a tailgate party or eating inside their cars, pickup trucks interspersed with limousines.

Eleven A.M., the VFW hall. Dennis Keuter has wandered out from the card game going on in a back room to check on his briskets. He's pointing out his babies and indicating their final destinations. "These we'll eat today, these three go to a birthday party on Tuesday." All the pieces of meat have been trimmed to a grilling weight of seven pounds, and the extra fat is piled back on top. "That keeps 'em from drying out," Dennis advises.

Originally from Dunlop, Iowa, Dennis knocked around in the military for years. "I've been as far west as you can go until you start going back east," he says. A pipe fitter by trade, he left the service in 1981 to work in the petroleum industry in Oklahoma. "I came down here and drove a truck when the oil fields dried up." That was in 1985.

Keuter's lack of true Texas credentials hasn't kept him from attaining an unofficial title as the post's grillmaster. "Most of them don't know," he says of his Iowan origins. "To tell you the truth, I don't think they would really care. When it comes down to when they want something done, they come to me." He's even taking orders for Thanksgiving turkeys—prepared a little differently than the Pilgrims did, deep-fried in oil for two minutes a pound.

Dennis will smoke his briskets over pecan and hickory for five hours. As a transplant, he apparently has no allegiance to the traditional Texas fuel. "Mesquite burns too hot," Dennis says, "and it gives the meat a little too much bite." He does, however, believe in taking his Texas time. He'll give these puppies five more hours cooking in foil until "if you move them, they will fall dead-apart. Briskets don't cook fast."

Keuter closes the grill and heads back to the clubhouse through a fine drizzle. College football will be starting soon.

Noon, the Knights of Columbus. Jim Griffin takes a beer break. He knows it's time for a brew by the clock on the wall of his camper. It reads 5:05. Jim Griffin's clock always reads 5:05.

Griffin has been ignoring his brisket for a few hours, working on ribs and chicken and pork shoulder. Truth be told, shoulder is Jim's forte. He won first for this very un-Texan entry at the world championship in Meridian, Texas, using a recipe borrowed from Glenn Nickolas. The Texans' church of barbecue has been getting very ecumenical of late, according to both Jim and Glenn. Pork ribs have long been popular

It may seem odd that such a humble place is getting such a royal fete. LeMaster points out his version of a fire prevention system: a glass of water by the grill. "If that doesn't work we have a bucket. If that doesn't work we call 9-1-1."

(especially among judges) and shoulder is now something Texans are looking into. Paradoxically, beef ribs have never been very popular on the Texas barbecue circuit. But these Lone Star grillers aren't like their counterparts to the east who are so hooked on hog as to ignore other meats. There is almost nothing they won't cook.

Goat is becoming increasingly popular. Out in Brady, in the west-central part of the state, Glenn says, they raise a lot of them. So these fellows cook 'em. There's now a

bison world championship held in Santa Ana, he adds. They cook buffalo meat shipped in frozen from Colorado. Glenn plans to go to a wild hog world championship the next weekend. They let hogs run wild "over yonder," Jim explains, pointing in the general direction of the West. They round up the lean version of pigs about a week before the contest. These are not by any stretch some of the more exotic

meats they cook down in Texas. Ostrich and emu are now the subject of some contests in the Lone Star State, Glenn says, especially since some local entrepreneurs went broke raising ostrich and sold them off cheap.

For these guys, it keeps coming back to brisket cooked with mesquite, though. In fact, the buffalo contest is played out with just that—bison brisket. A lot of cookers pile on beef fat to add moisture to the extremely lean meat. And the Texans feel that while they may still lag behind in the area of pork, there are none that can match their expertise with brisket. Glenn says that whenever he leaves the state for a contest, someone approaches him, asking how to cook the stuff. He's even given pointers and recipes to a restaurant up in Kentucky.

And now it's back to brisket as Griffin starts to unpack the stuff from its container to get ready for the judges.

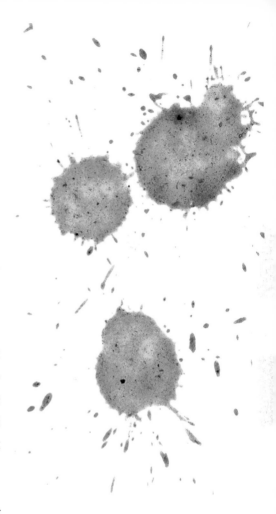

One P.M. at Sonny Bryan's. Business is really humming now as the counter people hurry to fill orders from customers backed up four and five deep. LeMaster says the staff here doesn't change very often. To get a job at the flagship restaurant, someone almost has to die. One of the customers at the condiment counter leans over and points to a waitress and says, "I've been coming here since this gal here was a virgin, and that's a long time."

Michael starts to enthuse in anticipation of the 40th anniversary party the restaurant is planning for the next weekend. Six hundred people are coming to eat "Q" and listen to Jerry Jeff Walker play. Naturally, it's sold out, and he says they're going to raise a pretty penny for charity—the local PBS station—between the admission fee and the auction-off. They're even going to sell off the tree stumps that people used to sit on outside the store.

It may seem odd that such a humble place is getting such a royal fete. LeMaster points out his version of a fire-prevention system: a glass of water by the grill. "If that doesn't work, we have a bucket. If that doesn't work we call 9-1-1." The electrical system is almost as antiquated, he says. "The lights flicker when you run a credit card through the machine."

Two P.M., Odom's BBQ. Not too many blocks away from Sonny's, Odom's occupies a more modern and brighter building, but there is no less sense of tradition here. Aaron Odom is in charge this day, at the restaurant started in the '60s; his aunt and uncle first called it Hardeman's. When Aaron and eight brothers and sisters took over in 1989, they changed the name in honor of their father—also named Aaron.

Aaron is taking a break in a long day and reflecting on his career in barbecue over a plate of fried chicken. "We've all done other things," he says of himself and his siblings. "I worked for AT&T. I was a real estate broker. But I came back here. When we were younger, this was work. I didn't appreciate it. I didn't understand the pleasure of my efforts. Now I like to see people get pleasure out of my efforts." Like LeMaster, Aaron gets a kick out of seeing generations returning to his restaurant. The people he calls "the old heads."

Odom's is known for ribs. The ribs are cooked over hickory wood in an outdoor pit for two or three hours, depending on the weather. Because the pit sits outside, ambient temperatures can affect cooking times. Designed by his uncle, its shape was inspired by the ovens used in the Louisiana paper mills he toiled in before coming to Dallas. "It's hard to go into a heavily populated area with this, it smokes so much. But it has a unique difference: you don't have to bother much with the meat once you put it in. Most people tend to do too much to barbecue. Less is better. The difference is going to be the sauce."

Aaron excuses himself, gets up and walks past the sign that reads "No Concealed Hand Guns Allowed" to go back behind the counter and put what's left of his chicken in the refrigerator. It's time to return to his clientele.

Three P.M. at Sonny Bryan's. It's been a fast day for Michael LeMaster. He locks the door of his little barbecue restaurant and walks through the dining room, turning signs around in the windows. Now instead of a welcoming message, the public is greeted with bad news: "Closed—Out of Food—Go to Our Other Sonny's." He's served as many people as he had meat for, and now and it's time for a cold beer, a moment of reflection and then home.

Four P.M. at the Knights of Columbus. Jim Griffin's clock still reads 5:05 and it's time for another cold one. This time he has something to celebrate. He owns the plaque for the best brisket at the contest. But Jim is not crowing about his cooking skills.

"I lucked out," he drawls out in a kind of aw-shucks way. "There are a whole lot of people who can cook brisket a whole better than I can. But they weren't here. Hunting season started this weekend."

Asked about what lies behind his success, he jokes: "I owe it all to good clean living and Budweiser." He might add the infinite patience of Billie, who puts up with his "little hobby." Like when he decided to cook 550 pounds of ribs for the Dallas Cowboys at training camp. Or when he built the Blue Flamingo from scratch outside the house.

"You haven't lived," she rolls her eyes, "until you've had an A-frame trailer on your patio for a solid year."

"You see, barbecue is a family oriented activity," Jim counters. "Everything is fine as long as we are together. My whole deal is fun. I don't play golf. I don't race cars. If I win, it's gravy. My prize money will pay for my trip over here and the meat I've cooked."

So all is right with Jim Griffin. He'll have a few more beers, sleep on it and head back to Wichita Falls, the Blue Flamingo in tow.

Six P.M. at the VFW hall. The rain has let up and Dennis Keuter sneaks out to Bubba's grill to check his briskets. He peels back the aluminum foil on one, lifts it and sure enough it falls dead-apart. Time to eat!

It's been a fast day for Michael LeMaster. He's served as many people as he had meat for, and now it's time for a cold beer, a moment of reflection, and then home. As all regular customers know, when it's gone, it's gone.

Lamb & Mutton

BaaBaaQued Lamb Ribs

2 tablespoons maple pepper

1 tablespoon garlic powder

1 tablespoon salt

1 teaspoon chopped parsley

2 8-bone slabs lamb ribs, trimmed

Mint julep sauce:

$\frac{1}{4}$ cup cider vinegar

$\frac{1}{2}$ ounce bourbon

1 tablespoon sugar

1 tablespoon finely chopped mint leaves

Rub spices well into lamb ribs. Place, bone side down, on barbecue grill. Grill over indirect heat for 40 to 50 minutes, turn ribs and cook an additional 25 minutes.

Bring julep sauce to a boil and simmer for 10 minutes, stirring frequently.

Separate ribs and serve with warm mint julep sauce. *Serves 4.*

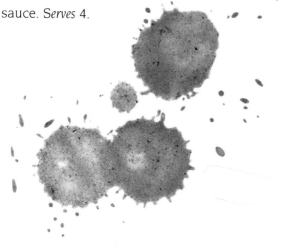

William's Huckleberry Meat Sauce

Pan drippings from lamb, mutton, beef, elk, venison or pork roast

2 small handfuls mountain huckleberries

$\frac{1}{4}$ cup red wine

2 tablespoons balsamic vinegar

Sugar

$\frac{1}{2}$ stick (4 tablespoons) cold butter, cut into pieces

Heat pan drippings in a saucepan and add huckleberries, red wine and balsamic vinegar.

Simmer, stirring, to reduce liquid and thicken sauce. Add sugar to taste. When sauce has achieved desired thickness, add butter and whisk until it is partially melted.

Put warm sauce into a sauceboat or spoon onto meat steaks. *Makes about 1 cup.*

Bill Kelley, Vancouver, Washington
This recipe was developed by Bill and Paul King, using Washington State huckleberries (don't ask, they won't tell you where they get theirs) and Idaho Rocky Mountain elk, in Paul's Sante Fe, New Mexico, kitchen.

Allen Guest's Lamb BBQ

$\frac{1}{2}$ cup extra virgin olive oil

1 5-pound leg of lamb, boned and tied

Salt

1 tablespoon maple pepper

1 tablespoon fresh rosemary leaves

1 teaspoon chopped mint leaves

1 teaspoon chopped basil leaves

Mint sauce:

$\frac{1}{2}$ cup red wine

$\frac{1}{4}$ cup apple cider

$\frac{1}{4}$ cup chopped mint leaves

2 tablespoons fresh rosemary leaves

$1\frac{1}{2}$ tablespoons white vinegar

2 tablespoons sugar

$\frac{1}{8}$ teaspoon salt

Combine the mint sauce ingredients in a medium saucepan and bring to a simmer. Cook for 5 minutes, stirring frequently. Pour into a jar that can be sealed. Refrigerate for 30 to 40 minutes.

Rub olive oil into leg of lamb and sprinkle with salt, pepper, rosemary, mint and basil mixture.

Cook over water smoker at 240°F for $4\frac{1}{2}$ to 5 hours. When internal temperature reaches 140°F, meat is medium rare. Remove from heat, seal in foil and let rest for 20 minutes. Serve with room-temperature mint sauce. *Serves 6-8.*

Barbecued meat should "rest" in aluminum foil for at least 20 minutes after taking it off the grill. This lets the juices retreat into the meat and makes it easier to carve.

Take-Your-Time Leg of Lamb

1 5-pound leg of lamb, boned, rolled and tied

1 cup balsamic vinegar

1 cup red wine

½ cup olive oil

¼ cup paprika

2 tablespoons garlic salt

1 tablespoon horseradish

1 tablespoon onion powder

1 tablespoon ground black pepper

2 teaspoons chopped fresh basil

1 teaspoon fresh rosemary leaves

At least 2 days before you plan to feast, pierce lamb with a large fork throughout. Combine the other ingredients and pour over lamb. Store in a plastic bag and refrigerate for 2 to 4 days, turning occasionally. One hour before ready to cook, remove lamb from refrigerator and reserve marinade, allowing meat to sit at room temperature for 1 hour. Prepare grill to 250°F.

Cook over indirect heat (mopping occasionally with the reserved marinade) for 2½ hours or until internal temperature reaches 130°F for rare, 140°F for medium rare, 160°F for well done. Remove from grill and allow lamb to sit for 30 minutes. The meat will continue to cook and will reach optimum temperature (140°F for rare, 150°F for medium rare, 160°F for well done). *Serves 6-8.*

Not the Spice Girls' Leg of Lamb

2 tablespoons lemon juice
2 tablespoons olive oil
Butterflied leg of lamb, about 3 pounds,
4 garlic gloves, minced
3 sprigs fresh rosemary
$\frac{1}{2}$ teaspoon ground black pepper
Apple juice

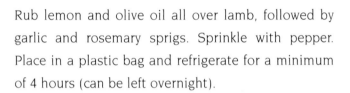

Rub lemon and olive oil all over lamb, followed by garlic and rosemary sprigs. Sprinkle with pepper. Place in a plastic bag and refrigerate for a minimum of 4 hours (can be left overnight).

Grill for 30 minutes on each side or until cooked to an internal temperature of 140°F (rare) to 160°F (well done). Baste regularly with apple juice (use a spray bottle to spritz it on). When meat has reached the proper temperature, wrap it in two layers of heavy-duty foil and set aside for 30 minutes so juices can be reabsorbed. Particularly good with huckleberry sauce (*see page* 136). *Serves 6-8.*

When you get tired of all the tongue-numbing spices in most barbecue recipes, you might want to back off to something more delicate, such as this one for butterflied leg of lamb.

Ten thousand volunteers help make the Houston Livestock Show and Rodeo one of BBQ's biggest events. More than a half-million hungry visitors come each year to indulge in world-class brisket.

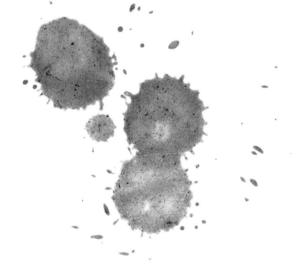

Kentucky Burgoo

3 pounds each: lamb, beef, pork and veal
 meat, including bones

1 chicken, about 4 pounds

8 quarts water

1½ pounds onions, diced

1½ pounds peeled potatoes, diced

7 carrots, diced

2 red peppers, diced

2 cups chopped cabbage

2 cups canned corn

2 cups lima beans

1 quart tomato purée

½ cup Worcestershire sauce

1 tablespoon salt

1 tablespoon crushed red pepper

1 teaspoon Tabasco Sauce

Place meats and chicken in a large pot and add water. Boil, then simmer until meat falls from the bones. Remove meat and cool, discarding bones, skin and fat. Chop meat and chicken into pieces the size of a fingertip.

Return meats to stockpot and add onions, potatoes, carrots, peppers, cabbage, corn, lima beans, and tomato purée. Put heat on medium and cook until thickened. Add seasonings and reduce heat to a simmer.

Simmer 10 hours, stirring occasionally. Mixture must be stirred constantly during the last 2 hours of cooking. Serve in large bowls for a hearty meal that will stick to your ribs.

Extremely labor-intensive (especially the last 2 hours), but well worth the effort. *Serves* 10-12.

Smoked Persian Lamb

1 butterflied leg of lamb, about 5 pounds
5 garlic cloves, cut into slivers
Marinade:
3 pounds sweet onions, thinly sliced
32 ounces pomegranate juice
1 teaspoon garlic salt
1 tablespoon lemon pepper

Cut small slits in lamb and insert slivers of garlic throughout the meat. Place meat in a large plastic bag and add mixture of onions, pomegranate juice, salt and pepper. Place plastic bag in a large pan. Marinate 2 to 3 days in refrigerator, turning 2 or 3 times a day.

When ready to cook, drain the meat, reserve marinade and let meat sit in pan for 30 to 45 minutes until it reaches room temperature. Heat smoker to 200°F to 220°F and oil or spray nonstick cooking spray on grill. Pour reserved marinade mixture into water pan and add 4 to 6 cups water.

Place lamb in a very hot frying pan or Dutch oven and sear meat, turning, until it's tinged with brown. Then place on smoker grill and smoke for 40 minutes per pound. Temperature will be 145°F for rare, 155°F for medium rare. When meat is done, immediately seal in aluminum foil and set aside to let juices be reabsorbed. Slice and serve on a heated platter. Serves 8-10.

Owensboro Championship Mutton

1 6- to 7-pound mutton roast

Moonlite black dip:

1 gallon water

2 cups Worcestershire sauce

$1\frac{1}{2}$ cups vinegar

$\frac{1}{2}$ cup brown sugar

3 tablespoons ground black pepper

2 tablespoons salt

2 tablespoons lemon juice

1 tablespoon garlic powder

2 teaspoons onion powder

1 teaspoon ground allspice

Mutton rub:

2 tablespoons garlic powder

1 teaspoon ground allspice

$\frac{1}{2}$ cup ground black pepper

3 tablespoons brown sugar

2 tablespoons onion salt

Heat dip ingredients in a large stewpot or Dutch oven. Cook on medium-high for 15 to 20 minutes, then cool. Place mutton roast in a large plastic bag and pour in three-fourths of the dip. Refrigerate for at least 12 hours; 24 is better.

Bring smoker to 220°F. Remove meat from refrigerator and let sit at room temperature for 30 minutes. Drain and rub in mutton rub mixture. Place on grill and cook for $1\frac{1}{2}$ hours per pound or until internal temperature in thickest part of roast is 170°F. Cover meat with foil and let rest for 15 minutes. Serve chopped, shredded or sliced with remaining moonlite black dip on the side.

You can substitute a lamb shoulder for the mutton, if necessary, as mutton is somewhat difficult to get at most grocery stores or butcher shops. *Serves 8-10.*

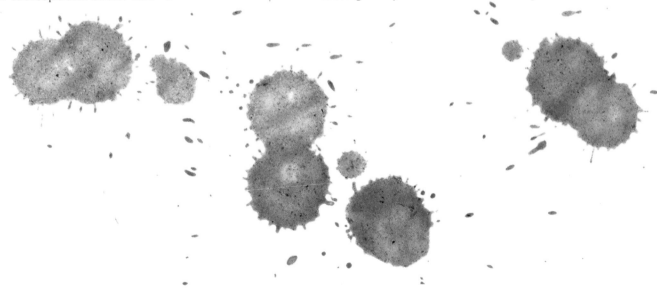

Beginning at midnight, teams at the Owensboro Bar-B-Q Championship fire up huge logs in 100-foot pits lining the downtown streets. Soon, 30-foot flames signal the start of one of America's most unusual barbecue contests.

Nevertheless, a fellow named Paul is standing his ground on the corner of Davies and First Streets in the middle of the Owensboro International Bar-B-Q Festival and calmly, but firmly, stating that they are all wrong. That this burg of 60,000 along the Ohio River is "the world capital of barbecue."

Furthermore, Paul bases his assertion not on the town's demonstrated talent for cooking beef or pork, but on a virtuosity with a meat that most people have only read about in medieval novels: mutton. Is this man out of his mind?

"No," says the self-possessed Paul in his overalls, boots and Lady of Lourdes baseball cap. He goes on to pronounce mutton the sublime medium for barbecue. Jaws may drop in Cow Country and Hog Heaven, but he's got a good point. Here's a meat, he notes, that's essentially indigenous to the area (Dutch settlers started raising sheep here some 200 years ago) and needs a lot of smoke to release its hearty goodness. Mutton is the senior citizen in the sheep family. As such, it takes more coaxing to surrender that tangy taste for which we revere his little brother, the lamb. Heck, Paul says that's why they sell so much of it at the Moonlite Diner out on West Parrish Avenue. They have beef, pork and chicken there too, but folks here know that mutton is the real show—the bulk of the ton of meat they go through every day.

The other part of Paul's case for Owensboro's predominance in barbecue stems from the very age of the event he is standing in the middle of. This may be the oldest barbecue festival in the country, as it can trace its roots back to 1834, when those same Dutch pioneers first started holding church picnics. And what do you suppose they cooked? It was in 1978 that it became a cookoff, putting it in precisely the same age frame as the vaunted Memphis in May contest. But as far as redneck picnics go, there is no contest. At more than 160 years old, Owensboro is a little higher on the hog, er, sheep.

To advertise its point, once a year in May (about a week before the folks in

Memphis have their own little cookout), the town quite literally fires up the streets. They build narrow cinder-block pits that run down the thoroughfares along the clay banks of the Ohio. They fill these grills with logs and set 'em ablaze. Flames leap 20 to 30 feet into the air before they cool enough for the smoking of mutton.

Truth be told, they don't only cook mutton at this contest. Folks do a pretty fair job with chicken and burgoo, as well. Burgoo is a meat stew that they've been making in this backwoods and blue grass music country since before the Boones and Lincolns roamed these hills.

One of the treasures of the Owensboro contest is the chance for noncombatants to join in the eating. Most of the cookers, many of them representing the many Catholic churches in the area, smoke much more than they need for the competition. The rest they sell for charity. And that's what brings many of the 70,000 spectators to Owensboro, Paul concludes. He figures he can score enough mutton, chicken and burgoo to lay up, reheat and feed himself for a month. You don't want to miss this day, he says.

People have their favorite "team" and line up, literally around the block, waiting for the appointed time when they can buy gallons of burgoo, great steaming hunks of meat and sizzling butterflied chickens. Informally, teams keep a record of how quickly their offerings are snapped up. This year the Lady of Lourdes team had more than 400 pounds of meat and 150 gallons of spicy burgoo disappear in minutes.

Charity doesn't end at the chow line. This festival includes beer gardens, road races, Soap Box derbies, karaoke contests, pie-eating battles, country dances and keg tosses, among lots of other extravaganzas. Most of them raise money for some charity or other. In the spirit of a time when candidates used to throw barbecues to lure voters to their rallies, there is even a political forum where local wannabes get to state their case.

Oh, and lest we forget that this town sits on the edge of the tobacco country, there is a tobacco spitting contest. Paul thinks he'll take a shot at it this year—once he gets fed.

Garlic Eggplant Grill

2 large purple or white eggplants

2 teaspoons seasoned salt

$1\frac{1}{2}$ cups olive oil infused with 3 blanched
   garlic cloves for 1 to 2 days

$\frac{1}{2}$ teaspoon Hungarian paprika

$\frac{1}{2}$ teaspoon freshly ground black or white pepper

Pinch ground nutmeg

Slice eggplants into $\frac{1}{2}$-inch slices (either horizontal rounds or bowling pin-shaped lengthwise slices); sprinkle with salt on both sides and lay in a colander. Wait 20 minutes to coax out bitter liquid. Pat-dry with paper towels.

In a glass baking dish, drizzle oil and sprinkle spices on each slice, then place slices, oil side down, on hot grill that has been lightly coated with vegetable spray. While cooking, drizzle oil and sprinkle spices on other side. Grill 10 to 15 minutes, turning the slices occasionally until they are tender, start to wilt and have some charred edges. Serve piping hot. *Serves* 4-6.

If you cut an onion and only use half and want to make the remaining half last longer, rub the cut surface with olive oil.

Bacon Corn Bread

4 slices smoked bacon

1½ cups stone-ground cornmeal

½ cup all-purpose flour

1 tablespoon baking powder

1 teaspoon baking soda

¾ teaspoon salt

2 tablespoons sugar

2 tablespoons butter, melted

3 eggs, lightly beaten

1 cup buttermilk

1 cup corn kernels (preferably fresh)

Flavored butter:

¼ pound (1 stick) butter, softened

2 teaspoons finely grated orange zest

Preheat oven to 400°F. In a well-seasoned cast-iron skillet, fry the bacon until crispy. Remove bacon, crumble and drain on paper towels. Save 1 tablespoon of the bacon grease.

Mix together the cornmeal, flour, baking powder, baking soda, salt, and sugar. When well mixed, add melted butter, eggs and buttermilk and stir lightly. Add crumbled bacon and whole corn kernels.

Swirl bacon grease around bottom of skillet and coat sides using a small basting brush. Pour batter into skillet and bake for approximately 20 minutes. The top should be light brown with the edges darker. Serve in wedges with a dab of orange butter on the side of each serving. *Serves 6.*

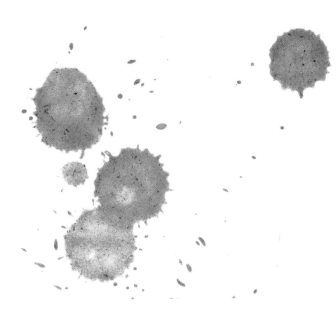

Christopher Robert Dennis Browne, USC,
School of Cinema & Television
A chip off the old block. Must have picked up
some talents from his Pa. Surprised us with this
recipe one Labor Day weekend picnic. He had
made both strawberry and orange butter. We all
preferred the orange. Wow, he can cook too!
Watch for his name at your local movie house.

Know Gud Rice

1 cup raw white rice
1 medium onion, finely chopped
1 medium carrot, finely chopped
1 medium red bell pepper, finely chopped
1 large stalk celery, finely chopped
1 tablespoon Worcestershire sauce
1 tablespoon steak sauce
$\frac{1}{2}$ teaspoon freshly ground white pepper
$\frac{1}{4}$ teaspoon garlic salt
1 tablespoon butter, melted
$2\frac{1}{2}$ cups chicken or turkey stock

Prepare water smoker and set temperature at 220°F. Mix rice thoroughly with all the ingredients except the stock and put in a cast-iron skillet. Cover mixture with stock and cover skillet tightly with lid or aluminum foil.

Place skillet on grill in hottest position in smoker and cook for $1\frac{1}{2}$ to 2 hours or until there is almost no liquid left in the pan. Uncover rice and cook for an additional 20 minutes until all the liquid has been absorbed and rice is fluffy. Serve immediately. *Serves* 4.

Unknown, Memphis in May Barbecue Contest
A woman who overheard me talking about this book walked up and handed me her recipe saying, "This has been in my family for 50 years and I'd love to share it, but my husband will kill me if he knows I'm giving it away." She walked off smiling. We were too after we tested it. Thanks Ma'am, it's terrific!

For a fairly mild, yet intensely flavorful pepper, try rocotillos—described as the best "eating pepper" in the world.

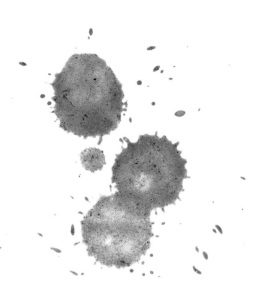

Smokin' Kebabs

4 red and green bell peppers, cut into 1-inch squares

1 large eggplant, quartered and cut into 1-inch cubes

4 Vidalia onions, cut into $\frac{1}{2}$-inch-thick wedges

12 cherry tomatoes

6 portobello mushrooms

1 large zucchini, cut into $\frac{1}{2}$-inch-thick rounds

$\frac{1}{4}$ cup corn oil

$\frac{1}{4}$ cup balsamic vinegar

6 large garlic cloves, minced

1 teaspoon dried basil

1 tablespoon chopped parsley

1 tablespoon chopped cilantro

Place all vegetables in a plastic bag. Mix oil, vinegar, garlic and herbs. Pour over contents of plastic bag. Refrigerate for 2 hours. Thread vegetables onto skewers, alternating types. Cook over medium heat for 20 to 30 minutes or until soft. Be particularly vigilant that tomatoes don't get too soft. *Serves 6.*

Grilled Tomato Soup

12 tomatoes, sliced OR
  6 tomatoes, sliced and
  1 6-ounce can tomato paste
$1\frac{1}{2}$ cups chicken broth
2 teaspoons chopped basil
2 teaspoons chopped parsley
1 teaspoon onion powder
$\frac{1}{4}$ teaspoon garlic powder
$\frac{1}{2}$ teaspoon freshly ground
  black pepper
$\frac{1}{2}$ teaspoon salt
2 tablespoons sugar
$\frac{1}{2}$ cup milk
1 tablespoon flour

Prepare the smoker for barbecuing at 180°F to 220°F, preferably burning hickory. Lay sliced tomatoes out on foil on grill and smoke for 30 to 45 minutes or until they brown slightly and start to wilt and curl up. Transfer directly to a large saucepan, trying to retain as much juice as possible. Over low heat, add chicken broth (preferably homemade from a bird you've smoked earlier) and tomato paste (if you choose method with fewer tomatoes). Allow to simmer for 15 minutes. Use wooden spoon to crush tomatoes and then transfer mixture to a blender or food processor to puree. Return mixture to saucepan on stove and add basil, parsley, onion powder, garlic powder, pepper, salt and sugar. Slowly stir in milk and flour. Don't rush the flour into the pan or you will end up with a clump of flour in your soup. Simmer for 2 hours, stirring occasionally. If you have squeamish guests and want the soup to seem like Campbell's, you can strain the seeds out, but then you lose some of the charm. *Serves* 4.

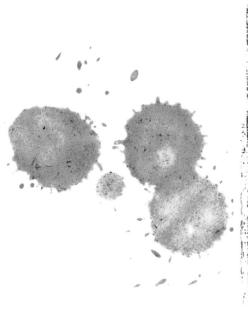

Uncle Grant's Sweet Taters

1 23-ounce can sweet potatoes, drained
   (reserve liquid)

1 cup buttermilk

$1\frac{1}{2}$ cups packed brown sugar

2 eggs, beaten

$\frac{3}{4}$ teaspoon ground cinnamon

$\frac{1}{4}$ teaspoon ground nutmeg

$\frac{1}{8}$ teaspoon ground cloves

$\frac{1}{4}$ cup pear cider

Topping:

$\frac{1}{2}$ cup packed brown sugar

$\frac{1}{2}$ cup melted butter or margarine

1 cup chopped pecans or walnuts

$\frac{1}{2}$ cup Grape Nuts cereal

$\frac{1}{4}$ cup golden seedless raisins

Preheat oven to 325°F. Combine ingredients and pour into a well-buttered 8-inch square casserole. Bake for 40 minutes. While potatoes are cooking, mix topping ingredients. Pour over dish and return to oven for 15 minutes. Serves 4.

Grant Cline Lawson Browne,
Kimberly, British Columbia
Older brother of the author, Grant was chiefly responsible for guiding him through the backwoods and forests of Northern Ontario and instilling a love of mother nature, which lasts to this day. Plus he's a heck of a cook, especially on camping trips where he first mixed up these potatoes in a Dutch oven.

Kara Beth's Spud Salad

4 unpeeled baking potatoes
4 sweet pickles, finely chopped
6 green onions, finely chopped
4 hard-boiled eggs, shelled and chopped
Handful fresh mushrooms, sliced
1 teaspoon sugar
$\frac{1}{2}$ cup yellow mustard
$\frac{1}{2}$ cup mayonnaise
1 cup sweet pickle juice
Salt and pepper to taste

Preheat oven to 350°F. Bake potatoes in skins for 45 minutes.

Dice potatoes and put in a large bowl. Add remaining ingredients and mix well. Cover and place in the refrigerator until ready to serve. *Serves 4-6.*

Cranberry and Port Wine Chutney

12 ounces fresh cranberries
$\frac{1}{2}$ cup sugar
$\frac{1}{4}$ teaspoon ground cinnamon
1 cup port wine
3 tablespoons slivered crystallized ginger

The night before you plan to serve, wash cranberries and place in a pot with sugar, cinnamon and wine. Bring to a boil over high heat. Reduce heat and boil gently, uncovered, until cranberries begin to pop, about 5 minutes. Stir in ginger. Remove from heat and chill. Refrigerate overnight. Keeps for up to a week. *Makes about 2 cups.*

CB's Smokin' Taters

1$\frac{1}{2}$ pounds potatoes

2 large onions

1 cup ketchup

1 teaspoon Worcestershire sauce

$\frac{1}{2}$ cup olive oil

$\frac{1}{4}$ cup paprika

$\frac{1}{3}$ cup packed brown sugar

Drippings from 1 pound of bacon
  (crumble bacon and reserve)

Salt and pepper to taste

Fresh parsley, for garnish

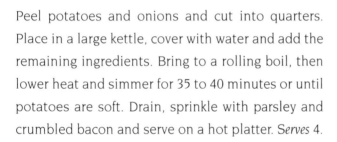

Peel potatoes and onions and cut into quarters. Place in a large kettle, cover with water and add the remaining ingredients. Bring to a rolling boil, then lower heat and simmer for 35 to 40 minutes or until potatoes are soft. Drain, sprinkle with parsley and crumbled bacon and serve on a hot platter. *Serves* 4.

Stuffed Baked Potatoes

6 large potatoes

$\frac{1}{4}$ cup finely diced onion

$\frac{1}{2}$ cup milk

$\frac{1}{2}$ cup shredded cheddar cheese

Salt and pepper to taste

Wrap potatoes individually in aluminum foil and bake close to heat on grill for 45 minutes. Sauté onion until brown. Remove potatoes from grill, slice in half and remove most of contents from potato skins. Mix milk, cheddar cheese, onion and potatoes and mash together. Replace potato mixture in skins and wrap again in foil. Cook for 15 minutes more on grill. Add salt and pepper to taste. *Serves* 6.

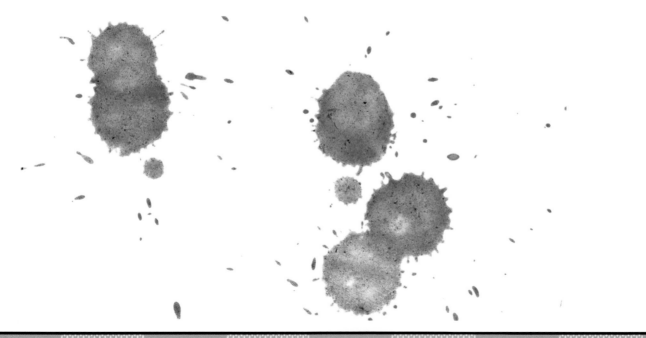

Rodney's BBQ Beans 'n' Bacon

6 slices smoked bacon, chopped

1 large onion, chopped into
$\frac{1}{4}$-inch pieces

1 medium red or yellow bell pepper

1 16-ounce can pork and beans

1 16-ounce can butter beans

1 16-ounce can baked beans

$\frac{1}{4}$ cup packed brown sugar

$\frac{1}{4}$ cup blackstrap molasses

$\frac{1}{4}$ teaspoon garlic salt

$\frac{1}{2}$ teaspoon maple pepper

1 tablespoon balsamic vinegar

1 tablespoon prepared yellow mustard

Preheat oven to 350°F. Cook bacon until it begins to be transparent. Add chopped onion and red bell pepper and sauté until soft. Add the beans and the remaining ingredients. Cover and bake for 30 minutes. *Serves 8-10.*

Rod Patten, somewhere in his truck,
somewhere in America
A truck-drivin' man, Rod first introduced me to his special beans in Salt Lake City, Utah. They are best served with garlic bread and spicy barbecue brisket. He once entered them in a barbecue contest in Fort Worth, Texas, but didn't win. Too bad for the judges—they missed bean heaven!

Baked Pineapple

1 can pineapple chunks

1 tart apple, peeled, cored
and sliced thinly

1 cup sugar

2 tablespoons flour

5 slices day-old bread,
cut into cubes

6 tablespoons butter

Preheat oven to 350°F. Drain pineapple juice and place in a saucepan. Place pineapple chunks in a shallow buttered 1-quart casserole and layer with apple slices. Bring pineapple juice to a boil and whisk in the sugar and flour and cook approximately 1 minute until thickened. Pour over pineapple and apple mixture. Pile bread cubes on top of pineapple. In the same saucepan, melt the butter and drizzle over the cubes. Bake, uncovered, for 45 minutes or until well browned. Delicious as a side with pork dishes. *Serves 4.*

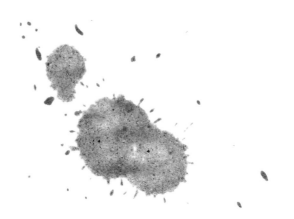

Just Peachy Pie

1 cup sugar
2 tablespoons tapioca
1 teaspoon cinnamon
Pinch salt
1 teaspoon lemon juice
4 cups sliced peaches
2 plain pastry shells
2 tablespoons butter

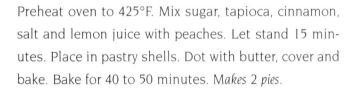

Preheat oven to 425°F. Mix sugar, tapioca, cinnamon, salt and lemon juice with peaches. Let stand 15 minutes. Place in pastry shells. Dot with butter, cover and bake. Bake for 40 to 50 minutes. *Makes 2 pies.*

Magic Cookie Bars

2 sticks (1 cup) butter
1 cup graham cracker crumbs
1 14-ounce can sweetened condensed milk
1 6-ounce package semisweet
    chocolate chips
1 3-ounce package flaked coconut

Preheat oven to 350°F. Melt butter in a 13 x 9-inch pan. Sprinkle crumbs over butter. Pour condensed milk evenly over the crumbs. Top evenly with the remaining ingredients. Press down gently. Bake 25 to 30 minutes. *Makes 20 bars.*

Carolina 'nana Puddin'

4 cups whole milk

6 eggs

$1\frac{1}{4}$ cups sugar

$\frac{1}{8}$ teaspoon salt

$1\frac{1}{2}$ teaspoons vanilla or Grand Marnier

Dash ground nutmeg

1 box vanilla wafers

1 pint whipping cream

7 large, firm bananas (with a touch of green)

Scald milk by bringing to a boil, then immediately remove from heat. In the top of a double boiler, beat eggs, half of the sugar and the salt. Stir milk into the mixture and cook slowly over boiling water until custard starts to thicken (approximately 20 minutes). Remove from heat, add vanilla and nutmeg and set aside to cool.

Line a large pie plate or a 13 x 9-inch glass baking dish with vanilla wafers. Whip cream at high speed until it forms soft peaks, slowly adding the remaining sugar and set aside.

Slice the bananas into $\frac{1}{4}$-inch rounds and layer on top of the vanilla waffers. Spread approximately half of the custard over the bananas. Spread half of the whipped cream over the custard. Add another layer of vanilla wafers, another layer of bananas, the remaining custard and the remaining whipped cream.

Refrigerate for several hours. Serve individual portions of the pudding and dot each one with a banana round or two. *Serves* 10-12.

Ol' South Pralines

1 cup buttermilk

2 cups sugar

1 teaspoon baking soda

$1\frac{1}{2}$ cups pecan halves

1 teaspoon vanilla

1 teaspoon butter

Combine buttermilk, sugar and baking soda in a large saucepan and cook for 15 minutes, stirring constantly. Add pecans and cook until mixture reaches the soft ball stage. Remove from heat and let cook for 3 to 4 minutes. Add vanilla and butter. Beat until mixture cools and drop by spoonfuls onto lightly buttered wax paper. Serve when cool. *Makes about 3 dozen.*

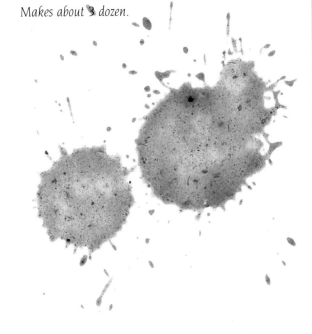

Grilled Stuffed Apples

4 large baking apples

$\frac{1}{2}$ cup raisins

$\frac{1}{4}$ cup currants

$\frac{1}{2}$ cup dry sherry or Marsala

2 tablespoons chopped walnuts or pecans

3 tablespoons brown sugar

2 tablespoons chopped maraschino cherries

1 tablespoon chopped dried apricots
   (soaked for 15 minutes in hot water)

$2\frac{1}{8}$ teaspoons ground cinnamon

$\frac{1}{8}$ teaspoon ground cloves

$\frac{1}{8}$ teaspoon ground nutmeg or allspice

3 tablespoons butter

Core apples, enlarging the hole with a grapefruit spoon or melon-ball tool. Place each apple on a sheet of heavy-duty aluminum foil. Mix the remaining ingredients except the butter in a large bowl. Spoon mixture generously into apples. Dot top of each apple with butter. Fold foil loosely and seal. Grill over low heat for 1 hour or until apples are done to your taste. Serve with vanilla ice cream (and caramel sauce, if you must). *Serves 4.*

Janeyce McCoy, Memphis, Tennessee
This recipe was entered in the Jack Daniel's Invitational
Barbecue Contest dessert category and placed fifth in fruit
entries. The Jack Daniel's is one of the only barbecue contests
in the nation that has a dessert category.

Mom's American Apple Pie

Pie crust:

2 cups flour

1 teaspoon salt

$\frac{3}{4}$ cup shortening

5 tablespoons cold water

Pie filling:

$\frac{3}{4}$ cup granulated sugar

$\frac{1}{4}$ cup packed brown sugar

1 teaspoon ground cinnamon

6 to 8 cooking apples, peeled, cored and sliced

3 to 4 tablespoons butter

Preheat the oven to 350°F. Combine the flour with the salt and cut in the shortening until mixed. Add the water and mix with a fork. Shape into two equal balls and roll out. Combine sugars and cinnamon and toss with apple slices. Pour into pie shell. Dot with butter. Cover with top crust. Sprinkle with cinnamon sugar, if desired. Lay a piece of foil over the pie for the first 30 minutes to avoid browning too much. Bake for $1\frac{1}{2}$ hours. *Serves 6-8.*

Carol Frye, Reno, Nevada

Dorothy's Sweet Cherry Pie

3 cups pitted baking cherries

$1\frac{1}{2}$ cups sugar

$\frac{1}{3}$ cup flour

1 teaspoon vanilla

$\frac{1}{8}$ teaspoon salt

1 unbaked 9-inch pie crust and dough for
   lattice-top crust

$1\frac{1}{2}$ tablespoons butter

1 tablespoon kirsch

Preheat oven to 425°F. Mix cherries, sugar, flour, vanilla and salt and pour into unbaked pie crust. Dot with the butter and sprinkle with kirsch. Cover fruit with lattice-top crust. Brush with cold water and sprinkle with a little sugar. Place pie on a baking sheet or a piece of aluminum foil, to catch drips. Bake for 35 to 40 minutes until top crust is lightly browned. Serve warm with homemade vanilla ice cream. *Serves 6-8.*

Dorothy, Texarkana, Arkansas
Winner of many midnight diners' hearts and famed in local bake sales, Dorothy was a pastry cook at a tiny, hole-in-the-wall restaurant I discovered on a college trip in 1966. Late one night, after a barbecue dinner, I fell in love with her pie and begged her to give me the recipe. She refused but took my address. At Christmas that year I received a simple card and a handwritten copy of her treasure: her cherry pie recipe. Thanks Dorothy. You're in my heart and stomach forever.

If you don't have any buttermilk, you can make your own in a pinch. Just sour regular milk by adding and stirring a tablespoon of lemon juice or apple cider vinegar to a cup of milk.

PARTY IN THE HOLLOW

Jack Daniel's Invitational: The World Cup of Barbecue

It's 6 p.m. in Lynchburg, Tennessee, and the last judges are straggling in for cocktails before the dinner at Miss Mary Bobo's Boarding House. Moore County has been famously dry since 1909, but the whiskey is flowing generously this night. After all, this little town of 361 souls is where Jack Daniel's is distilled, and even if the law says you can't sell booze, it isn't going to stop you from giving it away. Especially when the country's oldest distiller is holding its best party of the year: the Jack Daniel's World Championship Invitational Barbecue.

It's an invitational because each of the 30 or so teams entered has won some sort of major cookoff in the past year (a state championship is good for openers, but won't guarantee you a spot). It's a world championship because each year they invite a country from some far-flung place around the globe to send a representative to compete with the Big Boys of "Q." (Nobody really expects them to win, but it's a nice gesture and provides some work for the students from Vanderbilt University, in Nashville, who come down as interpreters.) And it's Jack Daniel's because, well, they're throwing the party and everybody seems to sample a little or find a way to slip some in a recipe here or there.

In the dooryard of Miss Mary's, it is like old-home week. This must be what it's like when they welcome inductees to the Hall of Fame in Cooperstown and all the baseball greats show up at one time. Karen Putnam, the Flower of the Flames, is there with her team Argosy. There is Joe Davidson of Oklahoma Joe's Hogamaniacs. His trademark grill, the shape and size of a steam engine, is already parked back in the hollow, where the teams will cook through the night and compete for world bragging rights. There's Slaughterhouse Five from Westwood, Kansas, led by Jim Howell, and the Pyropigmaniacs of Memphis under Bill Bryant. The Backdraft Broadcasters of Jackson, Mississippi, are also represented.

Inevitably, there are newcomers welcomed to the fold: Paul Schatte of Head Country II in Ponca City, Oklahoma, who traveled all the way to Tryon, North Carolina, to qualify at a state championship there. He was essentially alone—his wife came but was charged with taking care of the kids—and won anyway, even though his whole hog did catch on fire in the middle of the night in the grill he'd borrowed from a local just for the occasion. He gets a hearty welcome.

Then, of course, there are the overseas guests. A group of Teutonic cookers from Germany, Switzerland and Austria, with strange team names like Die Alten Baum, Roastis, Welser Wirte and the Swiss-Bull Grillers. They are getting oriented, but it won't be long before the southern hospitality and "y'all come in, now" spirit of this festival sucks them all in. These guys are along for the ride, to soak up some "Q" atmosphere and spread the word back home. But they don't have a shot in this crowd.

The smokers used at the major festivals can hold up to several hundred pounds of ribs, pork shoulders and even a whole hog.

It's a world championship because each year they invite a country from some far-flung place around the globe to send a representative to compete with the Big Boys of "Q." (Nobody really expects them to win, but it's a nice gesture.)

Lynne Tolley, the proprietress of Miss Mary's (she doesn't take in boarders anymore but still serves up a mean country supper starting every day at 1 p.m.), calls everyone to dinner, and the guests file into the old house. Hungry diners pile on fried chicken and other delicacies in the buffet line and proceed to the tables in one of four dining rooms. Talk abounds of contests past and whether anyone will be able to outcook the banquet set before them now.

Dinner done, everyone proceeds down to the hollow in a soft rain (it always seems to rain sometime or other at a barbecue contest). Carolyn Wells, the director of the Kansas City Barbecue Society and the ambassador of "Q," takes a microphone in the gathering under an open-air pavilion and introduces the dignitaries who will be judging. With us this year are Dorothy Mengering, David Letterman's mom and a regular on the circuit; Ardie Davis, a.k.a. Remus Powers, the poet laureate of "Q"; Charlie Vergos of the Rendezvous Restaurant in Memphis; Silky Sullivan of Sullivan's, also in Memphis; and Maxine Roberts from the Lieutenant Governor's Office. There are some folks from Jack Daniel's: Jimmy Bedford, the head distiller, who, it is presumed, knows a thing or two about tasting; Art Hancock, a retired bank vice president, down from Nashville; and Hank Terjen, a grandson-in-law of Lem Motlow, who took over the distillery from Jack Daniel himself. A handful of print and electronic journalists are down for the free pigout. Jim "Trim" Tabb, a distinguished cooker in his own right, is an unlucky alternate, hoping that one of the judges won't show, giving him a chance to manage.

The formalities done, the entertainment begins. The European guests show that they are in full spirit and lend their oom-pah, the Barrelhouse Gang clad in lederhosen, to the festivities. Everyone agrees it's nice of them to be so brave in the face of getting their patooties kicked tomorrow. Soon the crowd has given in to the evening, dancing away to the strains of accordion music.

Just as quickly as the party began, it is time for contestants to get back to their grills and everyone else to repair to the comfort of their hotel rooms. Alas, tiny Lynchburg can't handle the overflow crowd, and most have to travel 20 miles to their beds.

Early the next morning, everyone is back: either packed into the hollow or taking the distillery tour before the judging gets started. By now, the whole Lynchburg area citizenry has awakened to the import of this prestigious event, and hoards of people are pouring into town, straining its parking facilities and making their way about the town square.

There's plenty to do on this fair day. The Tennessee Rhythm Cloggers and the Fun Pack Dance Team put on a show with their lightning-speed feet on the square. Craftspeople are everywhere, demonstrating and selling their wares. Of course, there's food for those whose appetites have been ignited by the luscious smells wafting up from the hollow: sausage, biscuits, roasted corn, fried pies and baked goods. The requisite Jack Daniel's souvenirs are on sale everywhere.

Just enough hoopla surrounds the hollow to make it fun without the whole thing turning into some kind of tacky carnival: a carousel, a greased pole climb, butt bowling, pig, duck and goat races. The canines can also get involved with a "Country Dog Contest" that is not exactly American Kennel Club regulation. Prizes are awarded for best personality, being the "most laid back" and free-style tricks. Next door, they have a lawn tractor pull. Bands play in the gazebo off the town square all day.

At noon, the judges show up at the pavilion and begin the very serious, responsible and taxing business of tasting. Well, maybe not that serious!

If it weren't roped off, the entire crowd would be in there chomping and smacking. It does take some restraint, however. If a judge were to eat every bite of the pork ribs, poultry, beef brisket, whole hog and pork shoulder that came their way, they would be digesting two to three pounds of meat in a two-hour period. Some try, but it doesn't leave much room for dessert.

Part of being a judge is making it look like you're actually working as you take bites and make little pencil marks on computer cards before they are rushed off for the official audit. One of the Swiss guests who is a noncombatant is dressed in a chef costume and taking very exacting glances at each cut as it comes his way, measuring smoke rings and assessing textures. Come on! This is barbecue.

By 4:30 p.m., the whole mob scene has grouped around the gazebo in the town square just up the hill from the contest. There's a lot of hootin' and hollerin' and backslappin' as each team comes up to take its prize in its respective category. And then the unthinkable happens. First prize is announced for dessert. And the winner is...the Swiss.

Dinner done, everyone proceeds down to the hollow in a soft rain (it always seems to rain sometime or other at a barbecue contest).

Pineapple Upside-Down Cake

$\frac{1}{3}$ cup shortening

$\frac{1}{2}$ cup sugar

1 large egg

1 teaspoon vanilla

$1\frac{1}{4}$ cups flour

$1\frac{1}{4}$ teaspoons baking powder

$\frac{1}{2}$ teaspoon salt

Pinch ground nutmeg

$\frac{1}{2}$ cup reserved pineapple juice

Fruit topping:

2 tablespoons butter

$2\frac{1}{2}$ cups crushed pineapple
   (reserve liquid)

$\frac{1}{3}$ cup sugar

$\frac{1}{4}$ cup slivered almonds

Preheat the oven to 350°F. Cream shortening and sugar. When mixed, add egg and vanilla and beat until light and fluffy. Sift together dry ingredients, and add slowly to beaten mixture. Add the reserved pineapple juice.

In a 9-inch pie pan, melt the butter. Mix the pineapple, sugar and slivered almonds. Pour into pie pan. Spread cake batter over the topping. Bake for 45 to 50 minutes until bottom of cake is lightly browned. Remove cake from oven and let cool for 4 to 6 minutes, then carefully invert over serving plate and serve. *Serves 6-8.*

A pinch of baking soda mixed in with frosting made with confectioners' sugar keeps the frosting from hardening.

Spicy Oatmeal Cookies

1 cup shortening

1 cup sugar

1 cup honey

1 cup molasses

2 eggs

3 cups flour

1 teaspoon baking soda

2 teaspoons salt

1 tablespoon ground cinnamon

3 cups raisins

2 cups oatmeal

1 cup milk

1 cup nuts

Preheat oven to 375°F. Combine shortening, sugar, honey, molasses and eggs and mix well. Sift flour, baking soda, salt and cinnamon and stir into shortening mixture. Stir in raisins. Add oatmeal, milk and nuts. Dab onto cookie sheet and bake for 12 minutes. *Makes 7-8 dozen cookies.*

Tennessee Mudpie Cake

2 sticks (1 cup) butter

$\frac{1}{2}$ cup cocoa powder

2 cups sugar

$1\frac{1}{2}$ cups sifted flour

4 eggs, slightly beaten

$1\frac{1}{2}$ cups chopped pecans

1 teaspoon vanilla

Pinch salt

1 small bag miniature marshmallows

Frosting:

1 16-ounce box confectioners' sugar

$\frac{1}{2}$ cup half-and-half

$\frac{1}{3}$ cup cocoa powder

$\frac{1}{2}$ stick (4 tablespoons) butter

Confectioners' sugar, for garnish

Preheat oven to 350°F. Grease a 13 x 9-inch pan. Melt butter and add cocoa; stir well. Stir in sugar, flour, eggs, pecans, vanilla and salt and mix well. Pour mixture into prepared pan and bake for 30 to 40 minutes. While cake is baking, mix frosting ingredients and beat until smooth. Cover top of cake with miniature marshmallows while the cake is still warm and immediately spread the frosting over the marshmallows. Dust with confectioners' sugar. *Serves 10-12.*

Homemade Chocolate Sauce

3 ounces unsweetened chocolate

1 tablespoon butter

1 cup sugar

1 teaspoon vanilla

Pinch salt

1 cup sweetened condensed milk

Melt chocolate with butter in a double boiler. Add sugar, vanilla and salt. Mix well and gradually add milk. Boil for 5 minutes until smooth. Serve warm over vanilla ice cream. *Makes 1½ cups.*

Trisha's Crazy Cake

1 cup flour

1 cup sugar

1 cup cold water

6 tablespoons oil

3 tablespoons cocoa

1 tablespoon white vinegar

1 teaspoon baking soda

1 teaspoon salt

1 teaspoon vanilla

Confectioners' sugar, for garnish

Preheat oven to 350°F. Mix all ingredients well with a fork—do not beat. Pour into a greased 8-inch square pan. Bake for 20 to 25 minutes. *Serves 6-8.*

Summer Pudding

1 pound assorted fresh berries (strawberries, raspberries, huckleberries, etc.)

1 cup water

⅓ cup sugar

2 teaspoons lemon juice

6 slices white bread, crusts removed

Wash the berries. Place in a saucepan with the water, sugar and lemon juice. Cover and simmer over low heat for 10 minutes. Meanwhile, cut the bread into small shapes and line a round, 1-quart dish. Reserve enough bread for the top layer of the dish.

Strain the fruit and reserve the juice. Sprinkle one-third of the juice over the bread. Fill the dish with the fruit and sprinkle the second third of the juice over the fruit. Cover the fruit with the reserved bread and sprinkle the remaining third of the juice over it. Place a plate on top of the bread. Weight it down with a large can and refrigerate overnight. Carefully remove the pudding by inverting it onto a serving plate. Serve with vanilla ice cream or whipped cream. *Serves 4.*

Don't judge a barbecuer by his outward appearance. "Q" afficionados come from all levels of society and include doctors, CEOs, engineers, scientists, bankers, teachers and politicians. Even Vice President Al Gore has competed, cooking at the Memphis in May barbecue event.

Appendix

SMOKIN' WITH GAS

Forty-three percent of all barbecues are charcoal. The rest are gas. Some people have both.

Lock your doors before you start reading this. Make sure the children are in bed and the shutters are closed. In the realm of barbecuedom, what we are about to discuss is so heretical that it is not even open for discussion among "Q" fans. Polite grill society won't broach the subject. Even the most vehement arguments between Texans and Carolinians will never veer in this direction. It is off limits, verboten, taboo. It is barbecuing with gas.

You'll never see gas grills at barbecue contests (except where manufacturers are trying to sell their product). You never hear grillmasters discussing the merits of one propane-fired oven over another. Nobody ever compares natural gas to bottled gas. And yet gas grills are everywhere. They are among the hottest selling items in the grilling world. Somebody must be using them and it can't be just for hamburgers and steaks. Briskets and ribs must be finding their way onto those babies. Somebody must be breaking the cardinal rule of the barbecue: Never cook with gas.

Well, I'm here to confess that it's me. I'm guilty. I've been smoking with gas, and I'm proud of it. No more standing around meekly while the big boys talk about stoking up logs and flaming charcoal. I'm out of the closet.

And why shouldn't I be? What's so bad about cooking with gas (generally an expression of success in all other worlds besides barbecue)? Well, grill stars will give you two main reasons not to do it: 1) Gas imparts objectionable flavor to the meat. To start with, I don't believe it. Gas is one of the cleanest-burning commodities there is. Furthermore, if you can taste a little gas on a pork roast that's been marinated for hours, rubbed down with all manner of pyrotechnic spices, subjected to a smoke barrage and then juiced up with sauce, maybe your tastes are a little too rarefied for barbecue. Take your precious palate elsewhere, buddy. 2) Gas burns too hot for the low 'n' slow cooking techniques demanded in barbecuing. This is a stronger argument. While technically true, there are ways of fudging that or getting around it. More on that later.

First I want to talk about the advantages of gas—which are legion. The obvious one is ease of operation. You walk out on your deck, turn a dial, push a button, and— voilà!—you've got flame. Going hand in hand with ease is speed. You've just come home from a long day at the office. Do you want to start cooking now, or would you prefer to wrestle with charcoal and lighter fluid—then wait for it to burn down to the appropriate temperature? While we're on the subject of charcoal and fluid, how much does that stuff cost? You could go broke laying in a decent supply, and then you are likely to run out at the wrong time. For a fraction of the cost, you can keep a can of gas that will last for months, even when you cook regularly. Furthermore, charcoal is a messy commodity that sits around in a paper bag that eventually gets soggy and breaks up, spilling its sooty contents on everything. Meanwhile, gas waits calmly in its container underneath the grill, never spilling, never spoiling, and then when you need it starts right up.

So why doesn't everyone cook with gas? The answer is in the quick definition of barbecue: smoking slow and low. Gas is such an efficient fuel that it imparts none of these elements. That's where the fudging and jiggering comes in.

If you simply want smoky taste on your meat, that's easy enough. We've all seen the wood chips and chunks that are sold in bags in hardware, grocery and department stores. Simply soak the wood in hot water (higher temperatures open up the pores in the wood) for 20 minutes or more and sprinkle them over the lava rocks of your gas grill, and you'll have enough smoke to have the neighbors calling from blocks around. If you want to cook hamburgers or a nice tender steak this way, you can grill like you normally would, and the meat will come off with an interesting smoky flavor that will charm most and even fool some city folks into believing they are eating real barbecue. Or you could precook ribs indoors and put them on the grill for a little smoke bath at the last minute. While this is nice, it isn't the goal—for burgers and steaks aren't what real "Q" junkies call barbecue.

Barbecue is ribs and pork shoulder, brisket and skirt steaks, whole chickens and hogs (we'll forget hogs for our purposes)—big, tough cuts of meat that need to be broken, not just basted, with smoke. This takes cooking for hours—something that a gas grill isn't really made for. Why then use it for that purpose? Because, if you are like most citified or suburban "Q" fans, you probably don't have room on your deck or patio for the number of grills you'd want to satisfy every cooking need. You only have so much room in the corral, and chances are it's already being taken up by a trusty steed that eats gas.

Unfortunately, that gas grill you have isn't too subtle. It cooks at two speeds: hot and blisteringly fiery enough to burn the crud off the grill when you're done. How then to cook ribs for six hours and not come out with something that looks like the charred remains of a house fire? The answer is twofold: 1) keep the meat as far away from the fire as possible and 2) cook with the smoke, not the gas, as much as you feasibly can.

To achieve the first goal, you want a big grill that has many cooking elements. Most grills now have two controls, one for the left and one for the right burners. This is good. What is better is the multiple-burner grills that companies like Weber are now producing. You start only one burner, running as low as it will go, and then place your meat as far away from it as you can. (Since you are giving up half your real estate, you want to have three racks of grills to pile meat onto, as well.) Burn the wood chips or chunks (a word on that decision later) over the burner that is fired. Either place them directly on the lava rocks that come with many gas grills, in a cast-iron box (many grills now have one built in, but they can also be bought as accessories) or wrap them in aluminum foil with a few holes to let the smoke circulate out.

> The Smokin' Starlifters from the Tennessee Air National Guard have a smoker in the shape of a jet with a GCS (Grease Control System) in case "someone gets drunk and doesn't watch the fire."

There are two advantages to having the wood contained in a box or foil. Not being exposed directly to flame, the wood will smoke off slowly (which is what you want) while resisting flareups (which is what you don't want). Furthermore, when it comes to cleanup, you simply remove the box and dump it or chuck the aluminum foil pouch. Voilà, you've attained smoke and retained the cleanliness of a gas grill.

The wood comes in several different varieties, the most common of which are hickory and mesquite. Hickory is sublime. Mesquite, while having an interesting tangy

quality and an air of mystery to it for those not reared in the Southwest, has a problem. It burns a little hot (the very thing you are trying to avoid). One good way to overcome this is to mix it with a cooler burning wood. (It's a good idea to mix woods anyway to achieve flavor complexity.) Also sold are some other very respectable woods like oak, alder, apple and other fruitwoods. Availability often depends on where you live and what grows there. Smoking wood is also packaged in tin cans with small holes in them for placing directly on the fire. I've shied away from these because it's hard to get them smoking and because it removes the cook from the fire-starting process (which is, after all, half the fun of barbecuing, at least for testosterone-drunk men).

As to the choice of wood chunks or wood chips, I've found it's good to use a mixture. Chips will start smoking faster, which, when you're grilling something like a steak, is essential (you don't want the smoke coming on after the cuts are already done). They do, however, tend to flare up more than chunks, which will sit and smolder forever (perfect!) when you get the fire right. So get the smoke pouring off the chips, first, and then change over to chunks to get the job done.

I start the fire relatively high, let the lava rocks get hot and then put the meat on the grill (again as far away from the fire as possible). Put on the wood and wait until you get some whiffs of smoke, and then turn the heat down as low as it will go (this may take some jiggering with the control knob). The first blast of heat will open the pores of the meat and prepare it to take on smoke as it slowly tenderizes under low heat.

Now you want to keep the heat down as low as possible. It's best if you can rig a thermometer with a numbered readout as close to the meat compartment as possible. Some grills come with thermometers that indicate low to hot temperatures, but I don't trust them. On cheap models, low readouts tend to be hotter than you want to go. Either get a regulation grill thermometer or rig a candy thermometer to the grill (after a while you'll probably get so you can just touch your hand to the grill cover and know if it's too warm). Oven thermometers don't work because you have to open the grill to read them (causing the heat level to fluctuate) and because the glass on them will soon get too smoky and you won't be able to read the numbers.

Now, settle in to watch your fire carefully. (If you don't want to do that—and what barbecuer doesn't—this is not the method for you. Get an automatic smoker—like a Traeger—or simply cook indoors.) Ideally, you're trying to keep the temperature to 200°F. You might as well forget that. Think 250°F. If, after the wood is smoking, the temperature gets out of control, simply turn off the gas and let the meat cook on the fumes. If the temperature drops too low, start the fire again. If you're smoking the wood directly on the lava rocks, you'll find you can continue to pour chips or chunks on and keep it smoking without relighting. If the wood burns off completely, add more and relight the gas until it smokes again. I keep a long-nosed

In the last few years, barbecue contest judges seem to have acquired a sweet tooth. Mustards, honeys, and bourbon glazes are all finishing in the top categories on a regular basis.

grill lighter around in case the grill's igniter doesn't do the job right in the middle of a brisket. Most gas grills have holes (underneath the box and close to the gas burner) through which you can thrust a lighter or match to start burning again. (It is also good to have a backup canister of propane. It's a griller's nightmare to run out of fuel with the meat half done.)

Because some of the meat is always going to be closer to the fire than others, you must rotate it constantly to get even cooking. (You also might want to wrap the portions closest to the fire in aluminum foil.) With all this opening and closing of the grill (something traditional barbecuers are loath to do) you will have large temperature fluctuations, so it is important to monitor meat temperature closely with an instant readout internal thermometer rather than relying on cooking time alone.

Since you'll be adding wood throughout the process, it's easiest to keep a bucketful of chunks and/or chips at the ready. Also keep a spray bottle full of water to hose down any flareups that erupt inside the grill and threaten to char the meat. Again, this may seem like a lot of gear and fire tending, but that's what I'm in to.

With some practice, you should be able to work a shoulder or a bird for six or seven hours and approach the kind of tenderness they get at the competitions. Serve 'em up and, if you don't have to, don't let on that you didn't cook in a pit you dug yourself. And never, ever, show up with a gas grill at Memphis in May.

The amount of surface moisture in meat or poultry has much to do with pink color penetration. The pink ring is created when nitrogen dioxide (NO_2) is absorbed into the moist surface and reacts to produce nitrous oxide (N_2O).

CAROLYN WELLS

The Godmother of "Q"

Go to enough barbecue contests, and you're bound to see her. She's the one who seems to be everywhere at once, tooling around in a golf cart, talking on a two-way radio, speeding here, showing up there, solving problems, putting out fires (probably sometimes literally) and spreading love of "Q" wherever she goes.

She's Carolyn Wells, international ambassador of barbecue. In her capacity as executive director of the Kansas City Barbecue Society, she has done more than most to further the cause of "Q." Tirelessly promoting the art through a full schedule of contest organization and officiating, she also goes on television and radio and speaks to anyone (civilian and journalist alike) who wants to know about barbecue. Her organization developed the rules, blind-tasting methods and computerized tabulation that are THE standard of today's competitive barbecue world. She is seemingly willing to go anywhere to help out folks putting on a contest, and she does it with uncommon humor in the face of all absurdity.

Carolyn grew up on a farm in Missouri and remembers the days when her family would slaughter pigs in the late fall; she and her sibling would take off time from school to join in the festivities at home, which naturally included barbecuing pork. This love for barbecue never left her, and she found herself competing in cookoffs as an adult. It was in 1985 that Carolyn, her husband Gary, and a grill friend, Rick Welsh, decided over cocktails that the movement had become so huge and the demand for competition information and standardized rules so great that they would form KCBS. Soon they were putting on contests of their own and publishing the *Bullsheet*, the society's lively and informative newsletter. Carolyn, an accomplished pitmaster in her own right, has since given up competing, as she hardly has time for it. And besides, wouldn't it look suspicious if the woman organizing the judging brought home all the trophies?

Now that KCBS membership ranks in the thousands, Carolyn is fond of saying that they had only one rule when it all got started: Nothing could be taken seriously. That commandment seems to have lost its authority. "People who used to show up with pup tents and kettle cookers now arrive in motorhomes with all manner of elaborate equipment," Carolyn chuckles. "Some even have membership in the society listed in their obituaries. That's serious!"

Kansas City Barbecue Society, 11514 Hickman Mills Drive, Kansas City, MO 64134; 800-963-5227.

She is seemingly willing to go anywhere to help out folks putting on a contest and she does it with uncommon humor in the face of all absurdity.

BARBECUE SHRINES

The Best Places to Eat "Q"

The first thing you learn when you choose a life of barbecue is that "Q" hounds love to recommend restaurants. The farther out of the way and the more rundown the better. True believers take pride in how they've searched and suffered for the faith, and finding a place of worship that is remote and Spartan is one of the surest ways of going to barbecue heaven.

A typical barbecue recommendation goes like this: "It doesn't look like much and it's kind of out of the way, but they make great barbecue." The line is always delivered as though there is some great irony in the fact that an out-of-the-way place with no decor would serve good barbecue. Now, if you thought about it for a minute, that would be exactly the kind of place where you would be most likely to find great barbecue. "Q" joints don't charge enough for high-rent districts, so almost by definition they are going to be out of the way. Furthermore, wouldn't you be a little wary of any barbecue place that had chandeliers and linen tablecloths? Silverware and fine crystal would be suspect in a culinary world where menus and even waiters are often dispensable.

And so barbecues are most often known as rundown little shops with few amenities and not many selections. If they bother to print a menu at all, it is very likely to contain not more than one choice of meat, no sides and no desserts. Sometimes the menu is just a list of fare printed on a sign on the wall. Sometimes they forgo that luxury because the only thing you can order anyway is ribs (or shoulder or brisket, whatever the chef is most proficient at).

Simplicity is the soul of the barbecue restaurant. If sandwiches are offered, don't look for pumpernickel, rye or pita pockets. The perfect complement to barbecue is Wonder Bread (or occasionally a plain hamburger bun). White bread lets all the flavor shine through and soaks up the most sauce. Curiously, and for that same reason, white bread (served as toast points) is also the companion of choice for caviar (a culinary combination that could not be farther from barbecue).

Beverages are likely to be restricted to soft drinks and/or beer (again no rarefied microbrews here, look for Budweiser). Another beverage favorite is iced tea, which seems to have a sublime effect on the palate when mixed with barbecue. Strangely, the wine connoisseurs have never devoted much attention to pairing wine with barbecue, and so most "Q" joints don't have extensive cellars. If we had to guess, we would recommend full-bodied red jug wines with screw-on caps. Bourbon, America's other original taste sensation, also seems to go well with "Q" (at least, they down plenty of it on the contest circuit). It is hard to find in barbecue restaurants, however, because they so rarely have full liquor licenses.

More often than not, some of the best "Q" joints are found tucked away in unassuming cinder-block houses down a side street. Tables are likely as not to be picnic tables. It's not unheard of to find yourself sharing a table with another party. If there are tablecloths, they are the plasticized type that can be wiped clean with a sponge. Napkins are paper; sometimes a roll of paper towels is placed on the table (you'll learn to appreciate the gesture).

A contrasting restaurant design direction is barbecue baroque. Usually executed in shocking pink where pig is served, the idea is to memorialize the livestock you are about to eat in neon. The most popular image is that of the porker dressed in top hat, white tie and tails as he walks away swinging a cane and carrying a bag of ribs. This cannibalism motif was apparently first conceived at Leonard's in Memphis, in the '20s, and it has been copied by such notable temples as Gates in Kansas City. Another approach is to feature the smoker as prominently as possible. Smokestack, outside Kansas City, did the obvious and made its chimney prominent from far off. Bus Stop Bar-B-Q in Fayetteville, Arkansas, has a smoker ensconced in a school bus.

One final note: Don't be surprised by any customer mix. Barbecues are also usually egalitarian. While it isn't unlikely to see pickup trucks with gun racks in the parking lot of a good "Q" joint, you shouldn't be surprised to see Cadillacs and BMWs alongside. These people paid too much for their cars, but they are not stupid. They know good eats when they taste it.

Here are some of our favorite spots from around the country; just remember, some of these don't look like much and they may be kind of out of the way, but they make great barbecue.

Arkansas

Art's Barbecue and Catering (6901 Rogers Avenue, Fort Smith; 501-452-2550) Wedged in a strip of discount stores, Art's looks more like McDonald's than authentic barbecue, but let your tongue and not your eyes make the call.

Bubba's (Highway 62W, Eureka Springs; 501-253-7706) Among the tasteful Victorians of this old spa town, Bubba's fairly shouts barbecue with its shocking-pink color scheme and delicious sopping pork shoulder and beans.

H.B.'s Bar-B-Q (6010 Lancaster Road, Little Rock; 501-565-1930) Classic sparse design complete with linoleum tabletops. Most often recommended for its pyrotechnic sauces.

McClard's Bar-B-Q (505 Albert Pike, Hot Springs; 501-624-9586) This old family-style restaurant had a reputation for great "Q" before anybody knew who Bill Clinton was. It will still be around after Slick Willy is gone, whenever that is.

CALIFORNIA

Central Texas Barbecue (Downtown, Castroville; 408-633-2285) A hunk o' Texas in artichoke country? Yup, and a tasty hunk at that. With his cowboy hat, worn boots and long white hair, owner Don Elkins looks like a refugee from Texas hill country but cooks fantastic brisket, pork shoulder, links, and smoked turkey. The "Platter" is enough to feed three. Sawdust floor, steer horns and crowded dining rooms aside, probably the best barbecue on the California coast.

Memphis Minnie's (2800 20th Street, San Francisco; 415-647-7427) Hidden in the Mission District, Bob Kantor's restaurant/take-out provides real barbecue to San Franciscans. His ribs and shoulder melt in your mouth, taste like angels added the smoke, and cause local traffic jams.

COLORADO

Daddy Bruce's Bar-B-Q (1629 East 34th Ave.; 303-295-9115) Under the shadow of the Rockies, Bruce has brought world-class "Q" to Mile High. His dark, smoky, spicy ribs warm the coldest winter night. His sauce is "to die for" and features floating chunks of garlic, tangy lemon, ketchup, Worcestershire and vinegar, and a dry fire that you remember long after finishing your barbecue.

CONNECTICUT

Buster's Barbecue (1308 E. Main Street, Stamford; 203-961-0799) Given the address, this may sound like barbecue for preppies, but wait 'til you taste the "Q." Located right down the street from the World Wrestling Federation.

Kentucky

The Moonlite Bar-B-Que Inn (2708 Parrish Ave., Paducah; 502-684-8143) "A hundred thousand pounds of mutton a week," claims co-owner Ken Bosley. And considering that Owensboro isn't exactly a bustling metropolis, that number is incredible. But so is the buffet lunch, which consists of perhaps the best assortment of home-cooked food on the planet—and the best mutton you'll ever taste.

Starnes Bar-B-Q (Joe Clifton Drive, Paducah; 502-444-9555) Picture this: a U-shaped counter; a line stringing into a parking lot; a sandwich made from white bread, chopped pork, beef or mutton, grilled, and dotted with pungent sauce; and a bottle of cola. Instant nirvana.

Missouri

Arthur Bryant's Barbecue (1727 Brooklyn, Kansas City; 816-231-1123) Barbecue's gate to heaven—simple, packed, redolent of grease, sauce and plastic trays, but the best darn barbecue anywhere. Just ask Calvin Trillin. Their businessman's platter of barbecue meat is AWESOME.

Gates & Sons (4707 The Paseo; 816-923-0900) The logo has a fancy swell in top hat and tails, carrying take-out.

KC Masterpiece (4747 Wyandotte St.; 816-531-3332) Birthplace of the eponymous sauce.

The Grand Emporium Saloon (3832 Main St.; 816-531-1504) Proprietress Amazing Grace dishes "Q" and TLC to fans of rock-a-billy.

Smokestack Bar-B-Q (135th & Holmes, Martin City; 816-942-9141) A suburban grill with friendly waitresses and a smoky menu featuring everything but road kill.

New York

Virgil's (152 West 43rd Street, New York; 212-921-9494) We'll agree it's hard to find great "Q" in the Big Apple, but this is the real thing. The owners idolize Paul Kirk and worshiped at all the southern and midwestern shrines. You'll want to order Virgil's Platter. Don't unless you have a huge appetite, some help, or both.

North Carolina

Short Sugar's Drive-In (1328 South Scales St., Reidsville; 336-342-7487) Perhaps the best name for a barbecue restaurant in America. Serving up huge portions of pork shoulder chopped, sliced, or minced on a soft bun, seasoned with thin, tangy vinegar-ketchup sauce and topped with a big glop of coleslaw. Since 1949 they've served up legendary portions to anyone who knows barbecue and who comes from within a hundred miles.

Lexington Barbecue No. 1 (10 Highway 29-70 S.; 704-249-9814) The real "Barbecue Capital of America," Lexington features one barbecue restaurant for every 700 people in town, 18 in all, but this is the BEST. Their vinegar-pepper-ketchup-sugar sauce is the best of its kind anywhere.

OREGON

Doris' Café (352 NE Russell, Portland; 503-287-9249) Known across the Pacific Northwest for her "Rib Combo," a mix of barbecue pork and beef ribs, fried catfish, and sweet potato pie, Doris stands out among other pseudo-barbecue joints. Taste her ribs and you're in the South; a forkful of catfish and you're on the banks of the Mississippi; down some pie and you're humming "Dixie."

SOUTH CAROLINA

Sweatman's Bar-B-Que (South Caroline Rte. #453; 803-786-6455) South Carolina is yellow barbecue sauce country; yellow, as in mustard. This golden nectar, sweet and zippy, is spread on the pork and delights the taste buds of even the most finicky barbecue fan. Slow-smoked shoulders are drippingly moist and rank with the best we tasted anywhere in the country.

TENNESSEE

Corky's (*see page 205*)

Jack's (334 W. Trinity Lane, Memphis; 615-228-9888) Pork shoulder is incredibly tender; side dishes are world-class; brisket and chicken melt in your mouth.

Jim Neely's Interstate (2265 South Third St., Nashville; 615-775-2304) The birthplace of barbecue spaghetti, no less! The smell of "Q" hits you as you walk in, invading your hair, clothes and soul. Ribs and chopped pork on a bun are A+; barbecue spaghetti (pasta and barbecue sauce with burnt ends scattered throughout) is wonderful; desserts are worth the trip; and the ambiance is more than welcoming.

Rendezvous (*see page 204*)

There are more barbecue associations in Texas than in any other state; there are more barbecue festivals there than anywhere else in the nation, and citizens of the Lone Star State eat more beef brisket than anyone else in the world.

TEXAS

Kreuz Market (208 S. Commerce, Lockhart; 512-398-2361) This is the stuff of barbecue legend. A bare counter, butcher paper, sliced beef straight from the gods, a spicy sausage fit for an emperor, and, oh yes!, half a pack of saltine crackers, served up in a two-story, tin-roofed building 20 minutes north of San Antonio.

Sonny Bryan's (*see pages 122-125 and 127*)

Southside Market (109 Central Street, Elgin; 512-285-3407). Sausage king of Texas barbecue. They make "ropes" of sausage, cook them across a hot grill, serve them with an international orange hot sauce in whiskey bottles and dish it all up on butcher paper. Side dishes consist of crackers. That's it, crackers. But man, oh man, what sausages! All beef and all flavor.

Authors' note: Lest we be accused of missing a favorite Mecca for smoked ribs or mouth-watering brisket, we gladly acknowledge that the above-named restaurants, as well as those listed on page 206, are merely a token of the wonderful "Q" joints spread across the fruited plains of America. After all, there are more than 10,500 restaurants that serve up barbecue, and we wanted some room for recipes.

How to Tell if the Griller You Love Has Gone "Q" Far

He refers to barbecue as "the calling."

He plans to go to a barbecue contest on your honeymoon.

He looks longingly at the neighbor's Great Dane and wonders out loud how it would taste smoked.

He thinks rubs, marinades, mops and meat are the four basic food groups.

His will directs that his ashes be deposited in his grill with explicit instructions
for cooking his funeral dinner with his "burnt offerings."

He can riddle off whole recipes in minute detail, but he has trouble remembering the children's names.

You catch him singing, "Praise Father, Son and Holy Smoke" at prayer meetings.

He drives several hundred miles out of his way just to visit a particular "Q" joint—for breakfast.

He has joined a lobby group pushing to replace the eagle with the pig on all forms of currency.

He wonders if the neighbor's fence wouldn't make good charcoal.

You ask him for a nice back rub and he describes a mixture of paprika, sugar and chili pepper.

He owns more than five articles of pig worship.

He thinks Viagra is a new brand of meat syringe.

More than half the refrigerator is devoted to something called Really, Really Hot
I Mean It This Time Plum and Orange Sauce.

A spice chart gets more of a rise out of him than a Spice Girls' video.

He regularly gets into fistfights over which is better: tomato- or vinegar-based sauce.

ARTHUR BRYANT'S

Kansas City, Missouri

It's just an old brick building on a nondescript street in a quasi-industrial area of the city. Arthur Bryant's Barbecue Meats, 1727 Brooklyn Avenue, Kansas City, Missouri.

It's not much to look at from the outside, to be sure. Actually, it's not much to look at inside either, unless you're into Formica-topped tables and metal chairs cushioned in red plastic. Chairs you'd find and ignore at a garage sale. A few scattered plants sit in corners, some historic newspaper clippings dot the walls—and there's not an empty seat in the house! It's lunchtime at what many feel is barbecue's holiest shrine.

My pilgrimage to barbecue Mecca began, and ended, in the kitchen of perhaps the world's best-known barbecue restaurant. Called, not quite tongue in cheek (his mouth full of brisket at the time), by Calvin Trillin "the best restaurant in the WORLD," Bryant's has been happily dispensing ribs and brisket and spicy sauce to hungry crowds since the late '20s. Vegetarians need not

apply however, as the only vegetable matter served here are the potatoes, but they're fried in lard, and the world-class baked beans contain scrumptious morsels of the burnt ends of beef brisket.

Under the light of a yellowed menu sign hanging overhead, someone speaks. "Ham and brisket combo, extra sauce, fries and a draft," pleads a man who looks like he can barely contain his appetite long enough to pay for his lunch. The lanky counterman takes a giant handful of ham, drops it onto a slice of white bread, slathers on a thick brick-red sauce, covers it with another slice, piles on a fistfull of beef brisket, paints on more sauce, then completes the creation with another slice of bread. The huge sandwich, almost four inches thick, is surrounded by a huge pile of French fries and is then quickly passed to the nearly salivating man.

Meanwhile, other countermen and cooks scramble in the background, pulling mouth-watering slabs of ribs and sizzling briskets from the smoky oven, splitting chickens into tempting halves and dissecting slabs of ribs into large and small-end portions—every cut of meat having all traces of fat cut away before it is chopped, sliced and piled in pans ready to be assembled into their signature mammoth sandwiches.

They come to Bryant's, many call it "making the pilgrimage," from all over the world, but manager Eddie Echols' favorite patron is the Californian who chartered a private jet to fly there, piled $700 worth of barbecue into coolers, and then flew home for a party that night. For those who walk in, Eddie and his crew go through 600 pounds of meat, 500 pounds of potatoes, 300 loaves of white bread, 120 gallons of sauce, and 30 gallons of pickles every day. And on busy weekend days, ravenous clientele have been known to devour up to a half-ton of meat covered with more than 200 gallons of fiery sauce.

The kitchen and ovens are separated from the dining room by a large glass window. The sight of thick, glistening slabs of ribs, steaming sausage, succulent beef brisket, smoked turkey breast and drippingly-moist pork shoulder has an almost hypnotic effect on the line of people waiting to order. Those eating in the funky dining rooms grab their trays, the first available table they can find, and then attack their huge plates in a feeding frenzy. During my visit, one guy was so hungry he sat down and began tearing into a riblet sandwich before he realized he was at a table with strangers, not the buddies he came in with.

Four executives, their ties slung carefully over their shoulders to avoid being sauced, march triumphantly to a table carrying a tray piled high with pork ribs, sliced fragrant brisket, juicy pork shoulder, and smoked ham. A businessman's lunch here is defined as one to three pounds of mixed meats piled dramatically in the center of a plastic tray, drizzled with sauce, and accom-

panied by a half loaf of white bread, piles of fries cooked in lard (I know, I know—but they taste GREAT!) and zesty pickles. All to be washed down with frosty mugs of beer or, a local favorite, strawberry soda.

Essayist Calvin Trillin was once asked what were the best three restaurants in the world. His answer: "Arthur Bryant's, Arthur Bryant's, Arthur Bryant's."

"Orders-to-go," assembled on brown butcher paper, find the immense sandwiches, mountains of fries and tangy pickles rolled up lovingly into a package the size of a small football, disappearing out the screen door as fast as they can be wrapped.

Through it all, the smell of hickory smoke, barbecuing pork and beef, onion powder and molasses, vinegar and pots of baked beans, sausage and cumin, bubbling sauce and foaming brew overwhelm the senses. But at the end of what seems to be an endless line, orders are hollered into the kitchen, hands fly over platters of steaming meats, plates are piled high, and excited groans and a clanging cash register signal an end to the tantalizing wait. The pilgrimage has been consummated and nirvana is at hand, or, rather, fork. Please pass the holy grail of barbecue sauce and one more napkin!

But lest you think meals at Bryant's are absolutely perfect, there's one thing they don't have on the menu, so don't bother asking: There is no dessert here. There wouldn't be room!

No, it's not a hairdresser's controversy, or an argument for water rationing due to yet another El Niño (or La Niña) calamity. It's perhaps much more vital, visceral and vocal. It's the classic Memphis debate about how to cook, serve and eat pork ribs.

Wet—as in slathered with a red-hued sauce made up of equal parts of tangy tomato sauce and vinegar, seasoned with onion, peppers, honey, molasses and a passel of secret spices.

Dry—as in cooked over a grill then sprinkled with a dry spice concoction usually containing garlic, salt, cardamom, onion powder, paprika or just about anything else that is dried, powdered and edible, all of which give the finished rib a gritty, tasty crust.

The wet disciples, and they ARE disciples in every sense of the word, preach their gospel at barbecue pits, in restaurant waiting lines, smoke-filled bars and anywhere more than two people gather. "Their sauce coated every inch of rib," she gushes, "Every bite was heaven, the tangy complementing the sweet, the bite of cayenne smoothed with just a touch of lemon juice." She wipes her mouth on her sleeve.

Drys wax poetic when asked and are no less zealous in their preaching. "Never, never, never have I tasted anything better," the suit wails from the corner booth. "The ribs were unbelievable—falling off the bone, juicy and covered with a crunchy layer of spices which held in the moisture and offered a brief resistance to the tender treasure underneath. Never again will a dripping brush coat my 'Q' with sauce; I've found paradise! It's dry till I die."

THE "DRY"

Rendezvous: Memphis, Tennessee

Charlie Vergos' Rendezvous
General Washburn Alley, Memphis
901-523-2746
Tues. - Thurs. 4:30 p.m. - midnight
Fri. - Sat. noon - 1 a.m.
Closed Sunday & Monday

Wets head to Corky's, where they stand in line for up to three hours waiting to be ushered into a small, brightly lit restaurant. Drys seek an almost hidden alleyway entrance into Charlie Vergos' Rendezvous, the Mecca of the powdered spice sect, where there's seldom a wait—but then again, this gastronomic chapel has four floors!

Corky's is upscale, yuppish, jammed to the gills and features a neon sign flashing the portrait of a pig in a chef's hat. One hundred lucky diners can nibble bones at one time. Rendezvous is huge, multistoried, also jammed, and their only sign, in an alleyway off Second Street, one of Memphis' main drags, is small, plain and very difficult to spot. More than 1,000 people can chow down here simultaneously. Corky's is gleaming brass and polished wood; Rendezvous is barroom tacky with everything, including the kitchen sink, affixed to its walls, ceilings and hallways.

THE "WET"

Corky's: Memphis, Tennessee
Corky's
5500 Poplar Avenue, Memphis
901-685-9744
Sun. - Thurs. 10:45 a.m. - 10 p.m.
Fri. - Sat. 10:45 a.m. - 10:30 p.m.
Open Seven Days a Week

Charlie Vergos holds court at his Rendezvous. A place where ribs are cooked for several hours over an open flame, then quickly seasoned with Charlie's secret spice rub and served. Don Peltz, the seldom-seen owner of Corky's, has his ribs placed in a smoker and slow-cooked for more than eight hours over hickory and oak. They are coated with a spicy-sweet sauce and brought to the table.

By the way, lots of folks apparently like Corky's ribs, no matter where they live in the United States—Corky's did $5 million in business through FedEx last year and has its own FedEx office just down the road. Charlie Vergos has his edibles available via couriers as well, in addition to his sauces, spice rubs, aprons, hats, T-shirts and beer mugs.

Authors' note: Both styles of ribs are incredible. Wanna cheat? Go to Corky's and order their "half-n-half"—half your order is coated with sauce, the other half with their own "dry" paprika rub.

SOME MO' "Q" JOINTS

ALABAMA

Jackson
FRESH AIR BAR-B-QUE (fall-apart hams)

Northern region
GIBSON'S BAR-B-Q (outdoors)

Tuscaloosa
DREAMLAND DRIVE-IN (slabs o' ribs)

ARIZONA

Tucson
JACK'S ORIGINAL BARBECUE (blackened brisket)

ARKANSAS

Blytheville
DIXIE PIG (oldest barbecue restaurant in state)

De Valls Bluff
CRAIG'S BAR-B-Q (pork sandwiches)
PIE SHOP (Mary Thomas bakes the best pies in the South)

Little Rock
LINDSEY'S (founded by a bishop)

CALIFORNIA

Los Angeles
DR. HOGLY-WOGLY'S TYLER, TEXAS BAR-B-QUE (best brisket in Hollywood)
WOODY'S OR PHILLIP'S (cousins run competing barbecue stands)
FRANK NEELY'S INTERSTATE (brother of Memphis' Jim Neeley)

Oakland
EVERETT & JONES (best o' the Bay)

San Jose
ARMADILLO WILLY'S (not bad for a chain)

COLORADO

Denver
DADDY BRUCE'S BAR-B-Q (brought barbecue to the city)

CONNECTICUT

Stamford
STICK TO YOUR RIBS (authentic Yankee barbecue)

GEORGIA

Atlanta
ALECK'S BARBECUE HEAVEN (pork ribs and sandwiches)

Augusta
SCONYERS BAR-B-QUE (3,000 people a day)

ILLINOIS

Chicago
LEM'S OR LEON'S (great ribs in tough neighborhoods)

KENTUCKY

Owensboro
GEORGE'S BAR-B-Q (country's best burgoo)
OLD HICKORY PIT BAR-B-Q (2nd best mutton in the United States)
SHADY REST PIT BAR-B-Q (great barbecue pit)

MAINE

Portland
UNCLE BILLY'S SOUTHSIDE BARBECUE (French chef)

MISSISSIPPI

Clarksdale
ABE'S (pork sandwiches, smoked, in crusty finish)

Vicksburg
GOLDIE'S TRAIL BAR-B-QUE (beef brisket)

MISSOURI

Hutchinson
ROY'S (huge circular table where everyone eats)

Kansas City
BB'S LAWNSIDE (funky and flavorful)
HAYWARDS (owner Hayward Spears sells 9 tons of barbecue each week)
LC'S (open pit on street corner)

NEW MEXICO

Albuquerque
POWDRELL'S (side of chilies)

NEW YORK

New York City
THE HOG PIT (only other barbecue in New York worth it)

NEVADA

Las Vegas
MEMPHIS WORLD CHAMPIONSHIP BBQ (you roll 7's with their ribs)

NORTH CAROLINA

Chapel Hill
ALLEN & SON BAR-B-QUE (whole hogs in open pit)

Lexington
16 BBQ RESTAURANTS in a town of 15,000

OKLAHOMA

Clinton
JIGGS SMOKE HOUSE (frontier cabin pained with smoke)

Oklahoma City
LEO & SON BARBECUE (HUGE portions on dinners)
SHAWNEE VAN'S PIG STAND (oldest restaurant in Oklahoma)

SOUTH CAROLINA

Manning
D & H BAR-B-CUE (superb Southern barbecue)

Spartanburg
BEACON (skyscraper pork sandwiches)

West Columbia
MAURICE'S PIGGIE PARK (special mustard sauce)

TENNESSEE

Bluff City
THE RIDGEWOOD (Eastern Tennessee-style pork)

Mason
BOZO'S (draws fans from 100 miles away)

Memphis
LEONARDS (sign of pig in top hat and tails, superb sandwich)
BAR-B-Q SHOP (great bar made from confessional)
GRIDLEY'S (saucy ribs)
PAYNES (great pork sandwiches, mild smoke and robust sauce)

Nashville
JACK CAWTHON'S (superb pitmaster chops up a storm)

TEXAS

Dallas
THE PIG STAND (drive-in chain)

Fort Worth
ANGELO'S (huge barn)

Houston
OTTO'S (George Bush's favorite barbecue restaurant)

Taylor
LOUIE MUELLER'S (huge barn building)

Tyler
GREENBERG'S (smoked turkeys)

VERMONT

Putney
CURTIS' ALL AMERICAN NINTH WONDER OF THE WORLD BAR-B-Q (the best of Yankee "Q")

BARBECUE ASSOCIATIONS

California State Barbecue Association
Frank Boyer
2911 Bear Creek Way
Los Gatos, CA 95030-9497

Central Texas Barbecue Association
P. O. Box 4566
Temple, TX 76505

East Texas Barbecue Cookers Association
2709 Cedarcrest
Marshall, TX 75670

International Barbecue Cookers Association
P. O. Box 300566
Arlington TX 76007-0556

Kansas City Barbecue Society
Carolyn Wells
11514 Hickman Mills Drive
Kansas City, MO 64134

Lone Star Barbecue Association
Pat Nicholas
P. O. Box 120771
Arlington, TX 76012-0771

Memphis in May
245 Wagner Place
Suite 220
Memphis, TN 38103-3815

National Barbecue Association
P. O. Box 9685
Kansas City, MO 64134

New England Barbecue Association
P. O. Box 97
North Billerica, MA 01862-0097

North Texas Barbecue Cookers Association
P. O. Box 3024
Denton, TX 76201

Pacific Northwest Barbecue Association
Bob Lyon
4244 134th Ave. S. E.
Bellevue, WA 98006

Texas Gulf Coast Barbecue Cookers Association
26611 Weir Way
Magnolia, TX 77355

West Texas Barbecue Association
P. O. Box 5615
Odessa, TX 79764

FESTIVALS

TWIN CITIES RIBFEST: Minneapolis, MN

A five-day festival celebrating the glories of the barbecued rib draws more than 100,000 people to the city center of Minneapolis. When the barbecue circuit wends its way into the Twin Cities of Minnesota, it is time to get down to business. Literally. In a unique twist, this festival brings together 12 of the best rib restaurants (they call them "ribrateurs") in the country and lets them show the crowd how it is done by professionals. Not only will you get a lesson from the masters, but you'll be treated to Robinson's Racing Pigs, one of the more bizarre phenomena in all barbecuedom.

CALIFORNIA STATE BBQ COOKOFFS: Azusa, CA

The only major barbecue contest in America that features "Tri-tip," a tasty triangular section of top sirloin that is marinated and then grilled/smoked for up to six hours over fragrant wood smoke. The State Championship contest is held in historic Follows Camp, a scenic gold-mining camp on the east fork of the San Gabriel River, 30 miles from downtown L.A. and features recreational gold panning and dredging and a wonderful historical museum.

COLORADO BARBECUE CHALLENGE: Frisco, CO

There are bigger contests and older contests, but none are higher. Overlooking the Rockies at 9,100 feet, the Colorado Barbecue Challenge, now in its fifth year, has quickly become the place where flatland "Q" masters go when they want to cool off in the dog days of summer. Peek through the mountains, over scenic Lake Dillon, at this particularly homey contest west of Denver and see how high altitudes and idyllic scenery affect the crusty old smokers who come from all over in search of this prestigious state title. This 119-year-old community is indeed the place to enjoy mouth-waterin' barbecue and scenery, all in one juicy bite.

PUYALLUP TRIBE ANNUAL POW WOW & SALMON BAKE: Tacoma, WA

The Native American Puyallup tribe holds an annual salmon barbecue and festival, which is meant to preserve the native heritage of their forefathers. The tribal gathering also features competitive and tiny-tot Indian dancing, with 300 to 400 dancers and drummers participating, some from as far away as Canada and Alaska, and tribal heritage talks and prayers by their shaman. The salmon, freshly caught by tribal fisherman and unloaded each day, is both grilled over open fires and staked to alder wood to bake by the coals in the ancient way. Native arts and crafts and food booths offer tempting artworks and native foods.

BUBBA FEST: Spartanburg, SC

The barbecue circuit goes to the serene city of Spartanburg, South Carolina, for a stunning outpouring of southern hospitality. Not only will you learn how to do amazing things with every part of the pig but the oink, but you'll also see the folk arts of the back country, attend a Gospel Jubilee Concert and be witness to some hilarious Bubba Fest contests including: corn tosses, watermelon and pie eating contests (no hands), RC Cola chuggin' contests, and the Bubba/Bubbette beauty contest.

PIONEER DAYS BBQ COOKOFF: Fort Worth, TX

The real West, from historic reenactments to the National Gunfighter Competition, the thrills of Pawnee Bill's Wild West Show to the terror of bull riding at a championship rodeo. Stomp your feet to "push," "square dance" and "clogging" music or listen to country and western bands, then sit back and relax at a performance of the Cowtown Opry—all clustered around a barbecue cookoff contest featuring buffalo fajitas, turkey legs, jackpot beans, pork and beef ribs, and Texas' major contribution to barbecue: beef brisket.

ANNUAL NEBRASKA STATE BARBECUE CHAMPIONSHIP: Omaha, NE

Held in conjunction with Omaha's River City Roundup and Rodeo, the state championship is held alongside street dances, a livestock exposition and rodeo, trail rides and a downtown parade. The contest includes the normal KCBS categories but has a fifth meat category: beef top round roast, as well as side dish and barbecue sauce contests. Here in the center of America's beef country, you'll hoedown and party 'til the cows come home.

THE AMERICAN ROYAL: Kansas City, MO

America's barbecue Super Bowl. The competition fills two huge parking lots as more than 300 teams cloud up the Kansas City sky with hickory smoke. You'll see some of the "characters" of the art: Remus Powers, who dispenses his wealth of knowledge while wearing a bowler hat and an apron adorned with bones; Paul Kirk, the self-styled Baron of Barbecue; Karen Putman, the Flower of the Flames; and Carolyn Wells, barbecue's Godmother and its greatest promoter.

JACK DANIEL'S INVITATIONAL: Lynchburg, TN

If the Royal is the World Cup, then this is the Pro Bowl—as only teams who have won state championships are invited. There are thirty teams in all. In a town that makes one of America's favorite whiskeys, you'll spend time with the judges as they rate the "Q" put before them. Hobnob with the elite of the barbecue world, the legends of the coals, the barons of barbecue, the best of the best.

OWENSBORO BAR-B-Q CHAMPIONSHIP: Owensboro, KY

A visit to the world's largest whole sheep (mutton) barbecue on the banks of the Ohio River is as "down-home" as Memphis in May is "big city." Local charities convert the downtown streets into a smoky inferno by building 100-yard-long and six-foot-wide barbecue pits right on the pavement. Flames soar 30 feet into the air as teams prepare to cook more than 300 whole sheep (flavored with an ultra-secret black dip) and hundreds of gallons of spicy burgoo (the area's traditional barbecue stew).

MEMPHIS IN MAY: Memphis, TN

The largest barbecue competition of the season (*The Guinness Book of World Records*-approved) and what many people say is the best contest in the world. This is "Q" at its rowdiest. Two hundred fifty teams gather along the Mississippi in a celebration of pork-eating that lays down more than a mile and a half of smoke and features thousands of people wearing plastic pig snouts and tails, all trying to figure out whether ribs taste better dry or wet.

January

Cy Fair Go Texan Bar-B-Que Cookoff, Houston, TX
Hold 'Em & Hit 'Em Club, Houston, TX
San Antonio Livestock Expo, San Antonio, TX
Frontier Days Chili & BBQ, Breckenridge, TX

February

Bryan Main Street Project, Bryan, TX
Pig in the Park, Winter Park, FL

March

Hoots Annual Cookoff, Fort Worth, TX
Best Butt in Georgia, Moultrie GA
Batesville Ozark Hawg BBQ Championship,
  Batesville, AR
Rattlesnake Roundup, Sweetwater, TX

April

Rivergate Festival, Tunica, MS
Spring Pig Ribbin', Hawkinsville, GA
Hog Wild-Pig Crazy Barbecue, Lake City, FL
Blues & Barbecue, Savannah, GA
High Cotton Cookin', Greenwood, MS
The Greater Columbus Pig Jig Cookoff, Columbus, GA
Southaven Spring Festival, Southaven, MS

May

Esperanza Bonanza Barbeque Contest, Marion, AR
Shoot the Bull Georgia National Barbecue
  Championship, Hawkinsville, GA
Memphis in May, Memphis, TN
Owensboro Barbecue Cookoff, Owensboro, KY

June

Delta Jubilee-MS State Championship Barbecue
  Contest, Clarksdale, MS
Cookin' Up The Blues, Barbecue Cooking
  Benton County Barbecue Contest, Ashland, MS
W C Handy Blues & Barbecue Festival, Henderson, KY
Lakeland Funfest, Lakeland, TN
High on the Hog, Winchester, TN
The National Capital Barbecue Battle, Washington, DC
Show Me State BBQ Cookoff, Kennett, MO
Pig Fest, Richland, GA
Blue Ridge Barbecue, Tryon, NC
Great Lenexa Barbecue Battle, Lenexa, KN

July

Jimmy Dean Foods BBQ & Festival, Dyersburg, TN
Covington Jaycees World's Oldest BBQ Contest,
  Covington, TN
Holly Springs Kudzu Festival, Holly Springs, MS
Meat on the Mississippi Barbecue, Caruthersville, MO
Illinois State Barbecue Championship, Shannon, IL

August

Texas Championship Bison Cookoff, Early, TX
Alvord Watermelon Fest & BBQ Cookoff, lvord, TX
Whitehaven Hogfest, Memphis, TN
Nebraska Pork Producers/Capitol City Ribfest,
Lincoln, NE
Monterey Bay Rib Cookoff, Seaside, CA
Beaux Arts BBQ Cookoff, Jonesboro, GA
California State Championship BBQ, Azusa, CA
Wilson County Fair BBQ Contest, Lebanon, TN
Pawnee Bill Memorial Smoke-Off, Pawnee, OK
Musketaquid Summer BBQ Challenge, Concord, MA
Hoof 'n Hair Barbecue Cookoff, Jacksonboro, TX
Taylor International BBQ Cookoff, Taylor, TX
Garland Elk Sweeheart Yellow Rose, Garland, TX
Missouri State Fair Backyard BBQ Chef Contest,
  Sedalia, MO
The AHCT/F&M Bank Art of Barbeque, Tulsa, OK
Colorado Barbecue Challenge, Frisco, CO
Benton Co BBQ Contest, Ashland, MS
National Championship Barbecue Cookoff,
  Meridian, MS
North East National Rib Fest, North East, PA
Oregon Open BBQ Championship, Springfield, OR
Taffy Pull, Chili & BBQ Cookoff, Lajitas, TX
International Cityfest BBQ Cookoff, Tuscalossa, AL
Community Roots Festival BBQ Championship,
  Paola, KS

September

Crossroads Championship Barbecue Cookoff, Victoria, TX
Lago Vista BBQ Cookoff, Lake Travis, TX
World Championship Goat Cookoff, Brady, TX
Kentucky State BBQ Championship, Louisville, KY
Waylon's West Texas BBQ, Littlefield, TX
Chili & BBQ Cookoff, Odessa, TX
Hill Co. / Go Texan BBQ Cookoff, Hillsboro, TX
Bell Co. / Go Texan BBQ Cookoff, Temple, TX
Tennessee State Championship Cookville Cookoff,
  Cookville, TN
Brick Street BBQ Cookoff, Mt. Carroll, IL
Blue Spings Blaze-Off Championship Contest, Blue
  Springs, MO
Bubba Fest / SC State Championship, Duncan, SC
Hooves & Wings BBQ Cookoff, Hico, TX
Fayette Co. Hogmania, Sommerville, TN
Crossroads Annual BBQ Cookoff, Victoria, TX
Ohio Ribber BBQ Cookoff, Evansville, IN
National Cowboy BBQ Cookoff, Lubbock, TX
Cass Co. Missouri State Championship Cookoff,
  Harrisonville, MO
C & M Powder Puff BBQ Cookoff, Houston, TX
Mississippi State Championship / Benton Co.
  Cookoff, Michigan City, MS
Jessee James BBQ Cookout State Championship,
  Kearney, MO
Riverfest BBQ Cookoff, Decatur, AL
Octoberfest BBQ Cookoff, Frisco, TX
Cherokee Strip Bar-B-Que & Chili Cookoff, Ponca City, OK
Montague Co. Jubilee & BBQ Cookoff, Montague, TX
Waverly Apple Jubliee BBQ Contest, Waverly, MO
Carbondale State Championship BBQ Cookoff,
  Carbondale, IL
Best of the Beach & N.J. State Championship,
  Newark, DE

Pioneer Days BBQ Cookoff, Fort Worth, TX
Barnie McBee BBQ Cookoff, Comanche, TX
Smokin' By The Lake, Millington, TN
Nebraska State BBQ Championship, Omaha, NE
BBQ on the River, Paducah, KY
Connecticut State Championship BBQ Cookoff,
  Bethel, CT
Kinslow Chili & BBQ Cookoff, Amarillo, TX
Central California Tri-Tip & BBQ Chicken Cookoffs,
  Clovis, CA

October

American Royal BBQ Contest, Kansas City, MO
C & M Fall BBQ Cookoff, Houston, TX
Fall Fest BBQ Cookoff, Fort Worth, TX
Hog Wild in Corinth, Corinth, MS
Manor Lion Fest, Manor, TX
Pork, Beef & Chicken Cookoff, Brookhaven, MS
Big Pig Jig, Vienna, GA
Shawnee Great Grillers Bar-B-Que Meat, Shawnee, KS
Octoberfest BBQ Cookoff, Rising Star, TX
Heart of California Rib Cookoff, Riverbank, CA
Rib & Chicken Cookoff, Santa Cruz, CA
Pig & Pepper, Carlisle, MA
Traders Village, Grand Prairie, TX
Mountain Mania Fall Festival & BBQ Cookoff,
  Mountain Home, AR
Jones Co. Fair & BBQ Cookoff, Anson, TX
Fall Music & BBQ Festival, Coodlettsville, TN
Arlington BBQ Burnout, Arlington, TN
Bee Co. Area / Go Texan BBQ Cookoff, Beeville, TX
Southern Alabama Jubilee, Daphne, AL
World Championship Bison Cookoff, Santa Anna, TX
Ohio State Championship Smoked Meat & BBQ
  Festival, Nelsonville, OH
Water Valley BBQ Cookoff, Water Valley, TX
River City Rib Classic, Chillicothe, IL
Walker City Area Go Texan, Huntsville, TX
Lone Star BBQ Society Championship Cookoff,
  Arlington, TX
Jack Daniel's World Championship Barbeque,
  Lynchburg, TN
BBQ Cookoff, Fort Stockton, TX

November

Viva Terlingua World Championship Brisket Cookoff,
  Terlingua, TX
Ham Jam, Middleburg, FL
SW Mississippi BBQ Cookoff, Centreville, MS
Homebuilders Hog Happnin', Shelby, NC
Hog Wild in Hernando Co. / Florida State
  Championship, Brooksville, FL
Pig Fest, Richland, GA
Crowell Wild Hog BBQ Cookoff, Crowell, TX
Barbeque, Balloons & Blues Cookoff, Clermont, FL

December

Alabama State Championship, Demopolis, AL
Central Florida BBQ Festival, Sebring, FL

THANK "Q"S

We want to thank the hundreds of people all across America who have opened their hearts, fed us, provided us with cooling drinks to assuage the hot sun, and shared their most precious possessions with us: their recipes and how-to-"Q" tips. During our two-year pilgrimage in search of America's best barbecue, we discovered that there is no secret. It's the sharing, the friendship, the love of good food and family that make championship "Q" happen. Special thanks to Kathy Browne and Ellen Bettridge, our friends and our life partners, who put up with our kitchen experiments, tolerated our long absences, and knew just when to ooh and ahh at our recipes.

Amir Abdol, Corky's
Amy Corey, *Food & Beverage Journal*
Barry Bresnahan, Calhoun's at Rivergate
Bo & Pam Brinkoetter, B&P Hickory Pit
Bob Kantor, Memphis Minnies
Bob Lyon
Bob Swanson
Bobby Bishop, Bobby's Can Cookin'
Brenda Nelson, Rocklands
Brian Heinecke, NBBQA
Brian White, Red Hot & Blue
Brian Whittmer, Moose's
Burt Culver, Culver Duck Farms Inc.
Cammie Conlon, Mendocino Chamber of Commerce
Carlos Silva, Memphis Championship Barbecue
Case Dorman, Smoke Stack of Martin City
Charles D. McMurrey, Jr., Nottingham Internet Resources
Charlie Vergos, Rendezvous
Dan Russo, Virgil's
Dave Olson
Don Elkins, The Central Texan BBQ
Don Gillis, *National Barbecue News*
Donia Steele, Time Life
Doug Lanham, Famous Dave's
Ed Roith, Happy "Holla" Bar-B-Q
Eddie Echols, Arthur Bryant's Barbeque
Edward Kerins II, Lipton
Ernie & Phyllis Green, Meatheads Bar-B-Q
Frank Boyer, California BBQ Association
Frank Stewart, Smokestack Lightning
Hal Carmichal, Harold's Catering
Harry Neely, Jay Bee's Bar B-Que
Hayward & Eva Harris, The Rib Doctor
Hubert & Dollie Green, North Main BBQ
Inger Forland, Time Life
J. Russell Dillon

Jack Cawthon, Jack's
Jamieson Fuller
Janet Mathews
Janice Anderson
Jeff & Lynn Shiver, International Barbecue Cookers Association
Jeffry Erb, Back Forty Texas BBQ
Jennie Halfant, Time Life
Jennifer Pearce, Time Life
Jerry Coughlan
Jerry Tinsley, O'Tyme Hickory Pit Bar-B-Q
Jim "Trim" Tabb
Jim Burns, NBBQA
Jim Hogan, Strouds
Jim Neely, Jim Neely's Interstate
Jim Wodtke
Joan Marks, KCBS
Joe Duncan, Baker's Pits
John Frederickson, Curly's
John Potthast, Maryland Public Television
John Ross, KCBS
John Shiflet, Cookshack
John Snedden, Rocklands
John Vergos, City of Memphis
Joseph Bartush, Bartush-Schnitzius
Karen Adler, Pig Out Publications
Kathy Murphy, Ranch Hands
Ken Bosley, Moonlite Bar-B-Q
Ken White
Kyung Tai Rhee, Clean BBQ, Inc.
L. C., LC's Bar B.Q.
Larry & Tim Starnes, Starnes Bar-B-Q
Laura Godfrey, Natchez Convention & Visitors Bureau
Lewis Bunch, The BBQ Bunch
Linda Lichtendahl, Town of Frisco
Linda Shepard
Lola Rice, USA Smoke

Lolis Eric Elie, Smokestack Lightning
Lou Brancaccio
Martin Clain, Kansas City Barbeque
Mary Hammond, Paducah Convention & Visitors Bureau
Melanie Jones, Follows Camp
Merle Ellis
Michael White, Bar-B-Cutie
Mike Quillian, Mikes Pacific Smokehouse
Mike Townsley, Premium Standard Farms
Milan Chuckovich
Nick Spinelli, Jr., Kraft Foods
"Oklahoma" Joe Davidson
Pat & Glenn Nicholas
Paul Lee
Quentin McAndrew, Time Life
Rich Dye
Richard Alexander, Hasty-Bake
Rick Marshall, NBBQA
Robert Bishop, Blowin' Smoke BBQ
Robert Satterfield, Bad to the Bone Too
Robert Walker, Red Dog Productions
Ronnie McFarland, Bar-B-Cutie
Russ Matta
Sandy Hill Sweetser, Target Center
Scott Fine, On The Grill
Scott O'Meara, Boardroom Bar-B-Q
Sharon Rooney, Rooney Public Relations
Steve Tyler, Culinary Concoctions
Steve Tyler, Grill & Gourmet
Susan Stilwill, Fancy Food
Tana Shupe, Jack Daniel's Distillery
Terry Newell, Time Life
Tim Eidson, Mo Hotta Mo Betta
Tracy Satterfield, The American Royal
Troy Wayrynen
Vern Jackson, Frontier Buffalo Co.
Wynn Bellerjeau, Paul Revere Insurance Group

Index

TEST YOUR I-"Q"

Now that you've read the book, here's the final exam. Answer the multiple-choice questions and add your total below to see if you're ready for the barbecue circuit.

Pouring sweet tomato-based sauce all over a piece of meat and then grilling it at high temperatures is

A) The definition of barbecue
B) A surefire way to char the meat. Certainly not barbecue
C) Punishable by death

Memphis and Kansas City are

A) Two cities in the Midwest
B) The sites of two important barbecue contests
C) Locked in a mortal battle of barbecue to once and for all separate true believers from heretics

A barbecued whole hog

A) Is an obscene amount of food to cook at once
B) Is a good test of a grillmaster's talent
C) Feeds four

Stealing recipes from other grillmasters is

A) Despicable
B) Part of the competitive process
C) How I got shot

The film "Babe" is

A) Childish. Pigs can't talk
B) Groundbreaking. Finally a pig as the hero
C) Depressing. They never ate the pig

Hickory, mesquite and oak are

A) Three kinds of trees
B) The Grand Trine of barbecue smoke
C) My sons' names

Eating smoked meat in moderation

A) Is a one-way ticket to the cardiac unit
B) Can be healthy since the smoke breaks down the fat in the meat
C) Is for wussies. Barbecue is for breakfast, lunch and dinner

Vegetarians

A) Do not eat animal products of any kind and avoid wearing materials made from animal by-products
B) Can eat a number of grilled vegetables or seafoods and still maintain their vegetarian standing
C) Make good eating

Spareribs and beef ribs are

A) Interchangeable
B) Distinctly different taste sensations
C) Like matter and antimatter

Mops are

A) Kitchen implements for cleaning floors
B) Sauces used to baste meat while cooking
C) A good excuse to open the grill lid and mess with the fire

Barbecue is

A) Cooking outdoors
B) Highly spiced meat cooked slow and low over a smoky fire
C) A three-dimensional metaphor for life

Scoring: *Give yourself 1 point for each question answered A, 2 points for questions answered B, and 3 points for questions answered C. Give yourself 5 extra points if you got sauce or mop all over the test. Give yourself 10 extra points if at any point you considered using the test to smoke some meat.*

32 points or more—*Congratulations, Smoky, you're on your way to a brilliant career on the barbecue circuit—but do everybody a favor and shower once in a while.*

25 to 31 points—*Okay, Biff, you've got a chance, but watch that your coals don't get too hot.*

19 to 25 points—*Move your meat, Mike, your fire's starting to flare up.*

11 to 18 points—*Have another watercress sandwich, Tad, you're not ready for the "Q" world.*